Wintering Over

Other Books by *Joan Finnigan*

Finnigan's Guide to the Ottawa Valley:
   A Cultural & Historical Companion

Old Scores, New Goals:
   The Story of the Ottawa Senators

The Watershed Collection

Legacies, Legends & Lies

Tell Me Another Story

Wintering Over

JOAN FINNIGAN

Introduction by
Judith Thompson

Quarry Press

The publisher gratefully acknowledges the assistance of The Canada Council and the Ontario Arts Council.

Canadian Cataloguing in Publication Data
Finnigan, Joan, 1925–
      Wintering over

Poems.
ISBN 1-55082-049-4

      1. Legends — Ottawa River Valley (Quebec and Ont.) — Poetry.
2. Ottawa River Valley (Quebec and Ont.) — Poetry.   I. Title.

PS8511.I55W46   1992   C811'.54   C92-090449-1
PR9199.3.F46W46   1992

Design by Keith Abraham.
Cover photograph by Joan Finnigan.
Typesetting by Susan Hannah.
Printed and bound in Canada by Best Gagné, Toronto, Ontario.

Published by **Quarry Press, Inc.**,
P.O. Box 1061, Kingston, Ontario K7L 4Y5.

Contents

for Carl

Introduction

Every time I think of Joan Finnigan I feel grateful, for Joan was the first "lady poet" that I encountered. I remember feeling slightly nervous in her presence at first, because, being a child who lived to read, I believed that writers easily saw through all the mask and artifice to the wriggling, soft human beneath. But Joan quickly relaxed me, for it was clear that she warmly accepted and even delighted in whatever was underneath.

"Joan's Place" is about twenty minutes north of Kingston, Ontario, on Hambly Lake, far from the highway, deep in the woods. As a young child and later as an adolescent I visited her there with my parents many times. Joan is one of the few people I have met with a true interest in other people; I have often seen this interest bring out the best in people I know. She has always been a passionate and open woman. And all this "Joanness" runs like a river into her astonishing body of work. A body of work that for me, reaches its highest point in *Wintering Over*, her poetic/dramatic/historical celebration of the Irish/Scots Canadian immigrants of the early nineteenth century, but also including the voices of the French and the First Nations or, as the settlers called them, the "Indians."

I have always thought of Joan as quintessentially Canadian, and it's not just because she grew up in the Ottawa Valley and her father was a hockey star. Joan has always had the aura of a pioneer, perhaps because of the profound adversity she has faced, as a woman and as a writer, but also because of her passion for the land. I see Joan in these words from the title poem of this book, a dramatic monologue entitled "Wintering Over":

> I am here. This is me. Abigail Edey on the Ottawa
> in this log fortress, cradling a child in the snowdrifts
> of her husband's absence . . .
>
> I talk to myself and the child all the time, you know,
> and sometimes I just stand in the middle of the floor
> and yell out, "Where am I?" And the answer comes back,
> "You foolish woman!" You're not even on the map yet!"

Last year my seven-year-old daughter was asked to bring a "traditional food" to school for a celebration of cultural diversity. While other kids in her class took strange and exotic dishes, my poor girl was given a bowl of potato salad. I couldn't think of any Irish dish but potatoes. I was ashamed at how little I knew of my own history, despite my blood being Irish on both my mother and father's sides. I felt bereft, and rootless. Then I read *Wintering Over*. To read this stunning four-part work of oral history and human experience was finally to touch my roots. They are also the roots of many of the people I grew up with — descendants of the Irish, who fled the potato famine, or were brought over here as slave labour for the British, or who chose to immigrate to a new land, full of timber and wildlife and possibility. My ancestors, I believe were lucky enough to have chosen Canada, like Joan's ancestors described in "The Breakwater and the Web":

> My great-great-great gandparents here
> in Pontiac County, in Quebec, in Canada,
> not exiles but immigrants, not forced

by starvation out of an emerald country
despoiled by black potatoes, not shipped
by absentee landlords to the stony shores
of their native land and ordered
to leave — or die.

No. Choosers. The reins of their lives
in their hands. And I carry their decision
in my genes as surely as the moments of
conception . . .

To read *Wintering Over* was as necessary to me as was learning about the inside of my own body. And what a wonderful way to learn, not in the dry factual way we have become accustomed to in high schools, and universities, but through the passionate voices of individuals speaking/singing about their own lives, written with the hand of a poet.

The personal becomes political in many instances in this work, particularly in the dramatic poem "Songs from Both Sides of the River," in which the reaction of economic and class structures in this country is described plainly:

TOM: Now, Father, go back to 1840 for a minute. The
         Government of Upper Canada sold out all this pine
         country to all the aristocrats from the Old Country,
         Skeads, Conroys, Egans — people who came with lots
         of money to begin with. Then the second lot came in;
         J.R. Booth from Ottawa bought the Egan Estates at
         Madawaska in 1867 and Dan Maclachlin from Arnprior
         bought out Skead. In 1910 M.J. O'Brien from Renfrew
         there bought MacLachlin's limit on the Madawaska.
         They passed around the limits, you know. At that time,
         the limit-holders had the water-power rights too. M.J.
         O'Brien had limits he bought for twenty thousand

dollars and in 1929 right in the Depression — he sold
the water-power rights to Ontario Hydro for one million
eight hundred thousands dollars. That's one way he
made money — besides mining and railways.

Throughout *Wintering Over*, Joan Finnigan has let the voices of
the characters speak for themselves, neither judged nor censored.
This helps us to understand these Irish/Scots immigrants and
thus to learn a substantial amount about the origin of some of the
sensibilities of contemporary Upper Canadian culture, as seen in
these two passages from "Songs from Both Sides of the River":

> I've seen Telesphore Toussant, the Ghost of the
> Jocko River . . . at night he often came into the
> sleep camp through the roof. But after that the
> lumbercamp all fell into ruins and Toussant had
> nowhere to go but to the shores of the Jocko
> River — and that's where he wanders yet —
> and that's where I saw his ghost.

> I met her at church in Ste. Cecile de Masham
> — then I went off to a diamond-drill near
> Sudbury and she was waiting for me — and I
> came back with all the money saved to get
> married — and she was dead — died of
> appendicitis — I lay on her grave for two days
> and then I got up — haven't given a good
> goddamn for anything since.

Clearly Joan Finnigan has great compassion for these people, but
they are never romanticized. She unflinchingly reveals their bru-
tality:

> That was the worst day Calabogie ever saw. My
> grandfather McNulty said that the Irish was

walking up and down the streets, gathering,
arming with anything and everything. There
was going to be a Polish massacre. The women
were down on their knees praying and Father
Harrington was running from man to man . . .

But in the final section, entitled "The Breakwater and the
Web," the voice is Joan Finnigan's alone.

She speaks as a child of the Valley:

> In childhood everywhere we where we went in the Valley
> the arms held us, and wise men patted us on the head,
> knowing what we would become by the shape of our eyes;
> old wise women knew from watching for so long
> what was in our genes — "a Harper temper,"
> "a cowlick from the Cuthbertson's . . . "
>
> And we stood still, like cattle being judged
> at the Boyneville Fair, feeling uncomfortable
> because we sensed the judges knew our destiny —
> some for work, and some for war, some for racing,
> some for breeding, some marked for a return
> to the wilds or an early death, some to wander
> forever between two worlds, and only a few
> for true love.

I will return to *Wintering Over* again and again, to remind
myself that I am part of a "web," that I have an "old country,"
and that I do believe in ghosts.

Judith Thompson
Toronto, August 1992

Part One

Wintering Over

Wintering Over

I am here. This is me. Abigail Edey on the Ottawa
in this log fortress, cradling a child in the snowdrifts
of her husband's absence, alone in the middle
of concentric circles of desolation, fanning out
into the besieging snows — where went the footprints
of the Algonquin warriors, homewards to Calumet Island.

      See! On this home-made calendar
Cyrus carved in the sweet wood of loving care,
February 15, 1827. Five months I have stood guard here
in "Fort Abby" contemplating the wolves at the edge
of the clearing, they curious about these strange animals
with smoke coming out of their dens! And I, glad,
yes, glad of their company!

I talk to myself and the child all the time, you know,
and sometimes I just stand in the middle of the floor
and yell out, "Where am I?" And the answer comes back,
"You foolish woman! You're not even on the map yet!"

February 15. The sleigh haul in MacDonnell's camps
will be all over. The logs will be piled at the dumps
on the shore of the Bonnechere, waiting for The Drive
to begin in April. The men will be paid off —
Let's see now — Cyrus left October 1 — at thirty dollars
a month — that comes to $165 cash for the "cashless poor."

Cyrus made up a little rhyme for that:

> "Land rich and cash poor,
> But better off than ever before."

Yes, my beloved Cyrus, one of the best men ever was put
in this crazy country to try and get it started right —
Cyrus made this for me last summer on a lazy June day.
"Here, Abby, my girl," he said, "I don't want you to start
telling time by the moons — like an Indian!"
And we laughed together. But inside I was hurting
because I knew that after he harvested
all the potatoes, corn and wood,
he'd be leaving me here alone again —

I still don't know how — I still sometimes can't believe
that we pulled up from Randolph and came here
at our age to begin again. I have to be honest
and admit that one of the reasons we are here is to be
under the British flag. But that's not the main reason.
Oh, not at all! The main reason is the have something better
for our children than we were ever going to have
in that misguided Yankee melting-pot.
And I have to hang on tight to that, tight, tight, tight,
especially when I hear a wild west wind whipping up
a snowstorm from the river. I know I am about
to be tried again and I gird myself
in the invisible armour of will.

What does a woman do alone in a log house with a child
on the shores of a river she can't see for the trees?
Well, she keeps the fires going night and day,
I tell you that, for sure. And in this country
it's not only to keep the people but the potatoes
from freezing! Then you're down to nuts and artichokes —
and I've heard all about people having to eat their dogs!

Oh, we'd still be safe back in New England
but for the siren voice of that man, Philemon Wright.
And how might that have happened, you well might ask,
the Wrights being one of the big families of Massachusetts
and us just being simple Vermont farmers, trying to scratch
a living out of a little hilly farm — timber all gone —
for ourselves and Cyrus's widowed mother —
God rest her soul — and his younger brothers,
Daniel and Samuel?

Let me tell you that fairy tale:
Cyrus would go to Randolph regularly for supplies,
tea, salt, sugar, some wool from the woolen mill there.
And would you believe it? Wright used to come through
with his men on the way up to his new dominion in Canada,
and they'd stop at the tavern and the place
would fill up with men, discontented, listening to all
that talk of free lands, and waterfalls for mill-power,
and virgin timber waiting for a man to make his fortune.

For eight or nine years Wright passed through and left
behind him a trail of landlubbers sailing out on seas
of dreams. Cyrus's brother Samuel was the first to go —
and then the Chamberlains — and the Caleb Brooks —

The fairy tale ended.
And here I am. There's the bringing in of the wood.
You're a slave to that. You have to keep ahead of it.
An overnight storm can freeze in your wood
and then you have to dress — and leave the child —
and go out with an axe, and chop it free —
even if it is forty below and the wind is blasting down
from the igloos at the North Pole.
And you have to keep clearing the path to the woodpile
because a storm can fill it in. One time after a big storm
it took me two days to clear out my path
to the wood-pile. I was lucky with that one;
I have a good supply in the house but I was almost out
before I managed to tunnel my way through the snow
to the woodpile again.

Back in Randolph, Cyrus and I went as far as we could go
in school, eight miles there and back each day
up and down the high hills, and we both would have liked
to have gone further but our older people needed
us at home on the farm. My father got the Boston papers
and I devoured them — no — I memorized them! I knew
all about the Wrights and the high society people
of New England, half of them having come over
on the Mayflower. Or so they said. And we had a connection —
well, a little connection — my cousin Emmanda
married into the Choates — yes, the Washington Choates —
and one time Emmanda's mother, my mother's sister,
took my mother on her first exciting shopping trip
to Boston from where she brought me back a little diary
with a lock and key. "Here, Abigail," she said,
"You always like to write — and you were so good in school."

You ask me, what do I do here to keep from going mad? —
I've heard that some women do, you know — well, I tend
the child, and I hand-wring all the baby things,
I tell him stories, true and untrue, he doesn't understand.
I keep my diary both for myself and for Cyrus
upon his return to me — so we can laugh together again.
Isolation is so serious, so puritanical, so mirthless.
You can talk to yourself, sing to yourself,
read to yourself. But laughter must be shared.
That's why it's such a big big part of loving —

And I card and I spin and I keep knitting the socks
for next winter so Cyrus won't be crippled
like some poor shantymen by too thin socks
that lead to painful blisters in those big caulk boots
or Indian moccasins they always wear in the camps.
Imagine my Cyrus, a simple Vermont farmer, away up there
in the bush trying to cut down trees he says are as tall
as the Episcopalian church spire in Boston!

Joan Finnigan

Downriver, upriver, looking forward, looking back
I can see that, every year Wright and his men swept
through New England on their way up to Canada,
my Cyrus was more and more in the sway
of the come-hither call.

The first time he came to me, I screamed, "No, no, no!"
I was in a terrible mood. We had just lost a second child
at birth and I was to be tied to another little grave
in Randolph.

        "Why are all these foolish people leaving?"
I yelled at him. "They've cleared the land, built the houses,
the churches, the schools. In Woburn they walk
on board-walks through the spring mud, and some of them
even have inside water-closets! Why are they leaving?"

"Because it's something better for their children,"
Cyrus said, very quietly.

        "But we keep losing our babies?"
I screamed at him. And he walked away from me to the barn.
And stayed there. Until dark.

Then a couple of years later it happened,
right at our kitchen table in Vermont.
William Chamberlain stood up and cried out,
"Wright has taken the first raft of square timber
to Quebec! And sold it for enormous profit!
The old Quebeckers along the St. Lawrence told him
he'd never get by the Long Sault Rapids. But Wright said,
'I'll never believe that until I've tried it.' "

In the darkness of our little room upstairs
when the lamp was blown out, Cyrus put his arms around me
and came at me again. "I hear they are going to end
the free land grants in Lower Quebec," he said.
I did not reply. But in my heart I knew a wise woman
accepts it is to her advantage to be with a happy man.

Four weeks later I lost my third child a week
after it was born. To the day I die their little faces
will remain like cameos I wear on chains in my mind forever.
Cyrus wept. For a woman to watch the man she loves weeping
is to put all other things away.

"There must be something wrong with the air here,"
Cyrus said, as he was putting on his boots the next day
for the daily chores.

And I took him in my arms and said, "Whither thou goest,
I will go."

Let us not speak here of that unspeakable journey.
Seven weeks over ice and snow behind the patient oxen,
headed for the spring planting, me clutching my corn dolly
for good luck. And I finally met Philemon Wright,
a nice ordinary man who gave us good advice.
Cyrus, of course, was most anxious to take up his new land.
But Wright cautioned him. "Wait until early spring,"
he said, "when some of the snow is melted down.
Then you can see the lay of the land."
"But where will my family stay until then?" Cyrus asked.
"The land you will take up is above Aylmer on the Ottawa,
and there are several empty cabins along the trail,
left there by people who gave up and returned to Ireland.
Use one of those until you have built your own."
And then Mr. Wright turned to me. "And you already
have neighbours, Mrs. Edey," he said. "The Merrifields,
the McLeans, the Lusks are all up the river, and the surveyors
are going through to Onslow and Eardley —"

A day's journey from Wright's settlement we stayed over
at Symmes Inn in Aylmer. There we got the terrible news
of the Chamberlains —

But the air was good for us here. Matthew was born
in that abandoned log shanty we stayed over in
until our own house was built. Well, at least,
he didn't surprise us on the road up from New England!
But, since I had already lost three babies,
you can imagine the panic we were in when I went
into labour in that place!

And then this Indian woman fell from the sky.
Nobody heard her coming and nobody saw her coming
but suddenly she was at the door. "Me Alice Snowshoes.
Me help," she said. She eased my time with her own potions,
stayed with me and the child for a week afterwards.
Then she took Matthew in her arms, held him,
looked down at him, and handed him back to me.
"He's fine now. He stay," she said. And disappeared
across the River of Jordan for all I know.

"Now something better for our children!" Cyrus roared.

    "Abby, my girl," he would yell at me as he hitched
the oxen for another day of work, cutting, burning,
stumping, clearing. "I'll have you a view of that river
before you can say Witches of Salem!" And I smiled to myself
for I knew the river was a mile away.
"I'm just lucky to have a piece of sky," I'd yell
back at him.

Oh, don't ever be foolish enough
to think I'm never down-hearted here!
Sometimes on a cold clear winter's night when the wolves
are entertaining the moon, I people the dark wilderness
around me with all my neighbours. I pretend I see
the candlelight of the Merrifields upriver,
and the MacKechnies somewhere off there in the distance,
and the Walkers light downriver in that little shanty,
and then there's all those squatters far-off at the place
they call "The Springs" — the Dales, Hobbs, Armstrongs —
Yes, I set lights in my mind against all that darkness
like candles in the Christmas Eve Service in Randolph,
— and it helps me.

When I'm really down I think of Mrs. Chamberlain there
all alone in the wilderness with her seven children,
and her husband dead —

I must say Cyrus chose well, a beautiful flat piece
of land rivershore running back towards a ridge
that skirts the mountains — with even a meadow of beaver hay.
Some men from the Wright Settlement helped us build.
We had seen enough of log houses to know what we wanted.
It's bigger than most, sixteen by twenty-four,
with a log floor, laid tight and adzed smooth.
We made it high enough so that we can add rooms upstairs
and we built up on the ridge where the trail north
goes right by our door.

   "Close to company!" Cyrus laughed.
Looking back now, I wonder did he know from the beginning
he was going to shanty in the winters? Was he always
secretly planning on learning the lumbering business?

And I'll tell you another thing I do here;
I pray every night on my knees for my husband's safety.
Oh, he doesn't say much when he returns from the bush —
but I've heard from all the others about the men
who are drowned on The Drive, and caught in log jams,
and crushed by falling trees — the widow-makers.
I heard about a man from Hull who had his head cut off
by a cable — no, the only things much at all that Cyrus says
are things about the lumbering business itself —
"A log jam can ruin you — if you don't get it unhooked."
"When the logs don't get to market, you've lost everything —"

Yes, you keep the fires burning and you keep the woodpile
stacked high and close at hand. And you keep the water supply
open steady, not just for the people but for the animals —
they have to have water every day, too.

I keep my diary daily but there were two weeks
back in January when I couldn't write.
I know it had been a big storm in the night
by the way the house rattled and shook.
But it had all died down by morning when I opened
the door to go to the spring. The ice took me
straight down on my fanny.
Everything was glazed over with two inches of ice!
Lying on my belly I clawed my way back up hill
to the house, inch by inch, digging in my toes,
digging in my wrists until they were bloody —

It was like crawling through broken glass.
But I made it. I had to.

I'm still spinning on Mother Edey's spinning-wheel
all the wool we brought from the last sheep-shearing
in Randolph. Mother Edey — God rest her soul —
only lived a few months here after Matthew's birth.
But she had her life-wish; she did live to see
a grandchild. I don't know whether that long trip
was too hard on her or whether she just gave up
once she held the child in her arms. But she sickened —
and of course there's no doctor for miles —
and it was all over in two days. We buried her
at the edge of the clearing. That's another thing
they don't tell you about this crazy impossible country —
no cemeteries for Christian burial. Just a cross
at the side of the field. Cyrus says when he gets rich
he'll move her to a proper sanctified burial place —

I read the Bible aloud. And I get out
the hymnary and sing hymn after hymn. And I make
little phantom feasts —

Cyrus was away in the bush for his birthday —
November 5 — he was thirty four —

Yes, Cyrus was right again, about building near the trail.
Nobody ever goes by that doesn't stop in. We even had
a Reverend Bell from Perth who came by to say
a little prayer with us — sent by Mr. Wright he was.
Oh, how good that felt! To get down on our knees
with an ordained minister! Of course, it's not
the real thing, a real church sermon, with proper
Bible readings and everybody rising together to sing.
Dear God! How long are we to be in this place
without a church or a school?

As I was saying, nobody goes by that doesn't stop in —
surveyors, lumbermen, new settlers, the Assyrian pedlar,
strangers of all kinds —

I have a gun and I know how to use it!
I've never had to but I would — if I had to.

Speaking of strangers — that first year here I had
a "surprise attack." I was standing in the doorway
looking out when all of a sudden the clearing
filled up with Indians. I grabbed the gun from the wall —
but they were all smiling — and a couple of them came
right into the house and pointed to my newly-made bread,
fresh from the over. They had smelled it at the river!
I was so glad they didn't want us, I gave them everything
I had, and they went away like children with candy.

After the daily chores I am getting very good
at making up things to do. I invent new sock patterns
and I make up my own songs —
"Oh, my beloved, I have news for you —"
and I memorize parts of the Bible: I know all the Songs
of Solomon, and that beautiful one that begins
"Though I speak with the tongues of men and of angels —"
And I write down special thoughts in my diary
like, "One is less than one and two is more than two."
I wrote that one time when missing Cyrus came upon me
like a seizure in my whole being.

You know, you can smell spring in this crazy Canada
long before it bursts upon you, coming around a corner
from some other planet.

The surveyors who came through in January
they said this spring will bring many new settlers
headed upriver towards the free land grants
in Pendergast's domain. "Free lands only
for those who are Protestant," they said, and laughed.
And Pendergast stopped here, a big stern man.
He told me he was weary of all the fighting
in Ireland between the Protestants and the Catholics
and he was going to make a place on earth for peace.
That was his dream.

      "Where there is no vision, the people perish," he said.
"Proverbs, chapter twenty-nine, verse eighteen," I replied.

He arrived here on Christmas Day! Can you believe that?
And I was having another one of my phantom feasts.
I'd made a little Christmas cake, and cooked partridge,
and laid the table with all my Randolph linens,
and Pendergast came in as though some destiny
had sent him. After we had shared Christmas dinner
I asked him if he would sing with me, and we sang,
"Adeste Fideles," "Oh, Little Town of Bethlehem,"
"Away in a Manger." And then to save his reputation —
or mine — he slung his packsack over his shoulders,
put his snowshoes on at the door, and disappeared
into the Christmas night to bivouac down in the snows.
Poor man! If he'd only know it, he was as safe here
with me as if her were in the sanctuary of a church.
Besides, my contract of commitment with Cyrus
courses through my veins and is stowed in my gut —
sometimes I clutch the pillow all night long —

Like Pendergast, like Wright, like my Cyrus,
we are all dreamers here; I dream at night
of Cyrus's return and of going to Symmes Inn again,
of visiting the MacKechnies and the Merrifields —
making social calls like civilized human beings;
I dream of a new dress with a lace collar
so I can be beautiful for him — and yes,
there's a stone or brick house out there
with a guest room.

But mostly we are all dreaming of something better
for our children. And by that I mean *school*.
Not a church first, but a school . . . Oh, I do suppose
some people would think that's a terrible thing to say —
those Quebeckers, for instance — you can see
church comes first — we passed through their villages
on the way up from New England — huge stone cathedrals
surrounded by little tiny humble houses — like a hen
with chickens under her wings. But I know
from the Yankees and living near Boston
and reading Boston newspapers, and seeing all those books,
and hearing about all those Yankee children
sent off to private schools and boarding-schools,
and being tutored at home, I know that school comes *first*.

Now Cyrus, he wants roads first, and already
he's talking about going with Wright's men
to Quebec City to push the government there
for road improvements here. But I say *schools first.*
By the time my children are five
there'll be a school here or my name's not
Abigail Phoebe Fowler Edey.

As the eye of the butterfly sees only the flowers,
so the eye of Abigail Edey sees only the future
for our children, for our grandchildren.

I am here. This is me.
I've lived through another winter
alone in a log house on the Ottawa.
And I want to shout out
at this whole wilderness,
at this newborn uncharted country,
I may not be on the map yet
but I did it again!
You didn't beat me!
I've won another round!

I tell you I am not just a survivor here.
I am an achiever. For two years now
I have savoured that as an equal with my man.

"I may tell all my bones."
Yes, I'll hear him five miles away
coming towards me, snow-shoeing steady
like he heard a beat in his head,
and I'll be standing in the doorway
when he comes into the clearing,
and he'll know the minute he sees me —
he couldn't know before he left —
but I'll put on the blue dress anyhow —
the one he likes the best —
and I'll clasp him in my arms,
and I'll say to him,
"It is good for us to be here!"

"It is good for us to be here!"

The dramatic monologue Wintering Over *was commissioned by David Parry for the opening of the Museum of Civilization, Hull, Quebec, 1988. Since then it has been performed there almost continuously. The monologue has also been performed in many Ottawa Valley schools. Jennifer Boyes-Manseau was dramaturge and played Abigail Edey for the premier performances.*

Part Two

Cadieux

Cadieux

Cadieux, child magic out of March, came up
from Montreal, son of Jean Cadieux the First
and Marie Valade, offspring of the River
in the Year of our Lord sixteen seventy-one.

Why farm a long strip of boring habitant
when the forest was waiting to be taken?
As a young man Cadieux cast off the shackles
of his ancestral land. The preferable silence
of the woods was peopled with mysterious
indwellers — the unseen Walker in the Snow,
the loup-garrou and the windigos. Siren canoes
beckoned to unnamed lakes, discoveries of God
in unexpected places. The rich cargoes
of rare furs were freighted with dreams
of fortunes beyond silk and cinnamon.
And there were always the love lessons
of the Algonquin maidens in whom a secret
desire for a fair-skinned child ran
deeper than the tribal taboos.

Indeed, dalliance in a tent with Still Water
led to a tribal marriage on Calumet Island.
It was a good union. Indian women expected
their men to leave for long months at a time,
guided by Gitche Manitou out of the dark
lethal teeth of unknown rapids, the mouths
of the great carnivores. "Funny thing,"
Still Water laughed, "the polar bear is
the only animal that kills for fun —
and it is white!" Their half-breed bilingual

children were more Indian than French.
After all, their father belonged, not by birth
but by choice, to that immortal company
of coureurs de bois, white converts
to an acquired addiction for playing
with Death, fending him off with a flick
of the wrist.

Cadieux had spent the winter of the Year
of our Lord seventeen hundred and eight
with his Indian in-laws, snow-shoeing
around the trap-lines, tracking animals
for food, sleeping in the bear caves,
bivouacking in the boughs of pungent pine,
cedar and hemlock.

In March just before the break-up of the ice
Cadieux and his company returned by sled
to the camping-ground on Calumet Island
singing the history of a rich gathering
of pelts, the silk marten, the young otter
and the birch-fed beaver. For days
there was an orgy of fiddling, dancing,
feasting, and the wild-cat sounds
of reunion glee in the tents.

By May the Indians and the coureurs de bois
of the Upper Country had begun
to gather on the Grand Calumet,
preparing for the trip to Montreal
to sell or barter their winter gold.

One sweet cicely day in spring Cadieux
on the south shore beach was spearing fish
with his sons when an Indian runner burst
through the shore-line brush, shattering
the tender skies with the cry,
"The Iroquois are coming! The Iroquois
are coming! They are only three miles
down the River!"

All gravely came together at the camp-site.
"There is only one way to escape
from the Island and get down river,"
said Cadieux, "and that is to shoot
the rapids of the Grand Calumet."
All knew it as well as he. "Only one
has done that before," said old Silver Rock,
"and that was the great chief Antanewayway.
It was long before the time of the Moon
with the Black Teeth."

All standing there that day by the shores
of the Grand River knew that the Iroquois
killed everything in sight, sometimes slowly.
It was quickly agreed that possible death
by water was preferable to certain death
by flame.

"Someone must stay behind to attract
the attention of the Iroquois while the canoes
are escaping," said Cadieux, already

knowing with his sinking heart that the leader
must lead. "Who will come with me
and draw the invaders into the woods?"
Without a word, Footed Arrow, the swiftest,
bravest of them all, moved to Cadieux's side.

Quickly the canoes were loaded, the best paddlers
with their blades poised. "Remain close to shore,"
Cadieux ordered, "until I give the signal.
We will lead the enemy into the forest
by gunfire. When you hear the first shot,
set off down the river. God speed!"

The Algonquin paddlers silently held the canoes
on shore and waited. Then when the first gunshot
rang out, like possessed demons, they shot
their loaded craft towards the roaring cauldron
of the Grand Calumet, shot so fast
the fish swam into their mouths, shot so fast
they could not say when it was Saint Anne,
patroness of Quebec, entered the lead canoe.

Cadieux and Footed Arrow ambushed
the hostile Iroquois as they were descending
the portage around the Grand Calumet.
They killed four warriors and took to the woods,
firing many shots to delude the enemy
into thinking they were a horde of Algonquin,
instead of two lone decoys.

For three days and three nights the Iroquois
tracked the two men, finally killing Footed Arrow
and wounding Cadieux. He kept ahead of them.
When the Iroquois tired of the chase,
Cadieux turned for home. But his strength gave out.
Hungry, exhausted, bleeding badly, he dug himself
a small shelter in the hollow of a ledge
of rock, pulled some leaves and boughs
over himself and crawled in, hoping to recover
enough to continue his journey homewards.

Mother of the Virgin and wife of Saint Joachim,
Saint Anne stayed with the Algonquin canoes
all the way down river, around Devil's Elbow,
over the Chats Falls, past Rapides Deschenes,
the Chaudiere. By night, it was said, the halo
of Saint Anne lit the way.
She stayed with the canoes until they all reached
the safety of the Lake of Two Mountains.

Three Scottish voyageurs went into the woods
to search for Cadieux. They came so close to him
he could hear them calling out to him,
"Cadieux, Cadieux, where are you?" But, by then
he was too weak to answer or to move. As they
faded away into a final silence, Cadieux,
eyeless and voiceless, drank his own tears,
dreamed of Still Water and the beautiful children.

Some time later, returning to the Grand Calunet,
the Algonquin found Cadieux in his shallow grave.
In his hand he clutched a piece of birch bark.
On it, as painfully and slowly as his death,
he had scratched out his Death Lament:

"Fly, nightingale, to the dear ones I'm leaving.
Fly to my wife and my little ones grieving.
Tell them I guarded love and loyalty,
And to abandon any hope of seeing me.
Here, thus abandoned, I lie unrepenting,
And in the Saviour I have faith, unrelenting;
Oh, Holy Virgin, unfold your arms to me!
There would I lie for all eternity."

Part Three

Songs from Both Sides of the River

Songs from Both Sides of the River

SECTION I   *Beginnings*

MAN 1   Feathered,
           fringed
           beaded
           mocassined
           embroidered
           black-robed
           bonnetted
           tasselled
           ceintured
           sashed
           leggined
           capoted
           scarlet-toqued

MAN 2   bent to the paddle

TOGETHER   Our Father which art in heaven
           Give us the password to La Chine

MAN 1   the famished paddles carved
           the unknown turquoise seas

MAN 2   and we sought unwearyingly for the gateway
           to the unmined west

MAN 1   I, Champlain, up the Ottawa in a birch bark canoe
           with my Indian guides to look with my newborn eyes
           upon la Mer Douce

MAN 2　　And I, Joillet, down the great Mississippi,
　　　　　wondering as we paddled if we would fall
　　　　　into the Gulf of Mexico
　　　　　or the Vermillion Sea

MAN 1　　Voila! Here is the Holy Water route to Cathay!

MAN 2　　from dawn to dusk push west
　　　　　carve the untouched turquoise seas
　　　　　with your hungry paddles of dreams

MAN 1　　Brûlé, de Vignau, Champlain, Nicollet,
　　　　　Le Moyne d'Iberville, La Motte-Cadillac,
　　　　　La Salle, Du Lhut, Sieur de Coulonge,
　　　　　La Vérendrye

MAN 2　　turn north-west at the Lake of Two Mountains
　　　　　follow Main Street — the Mighty Ottawa —
　　　　　to Mattawa

TOGETHER　　Our Father which art in heaven
　　　　　Give us the divine divining-rod
　　　　　Grant us the open sesame

MAN 1　　And Jean Nicollet, expecting
　　　　　he would find the China sea,
　　　　　forged westward
　　　　　with a robe of Chinese damask
　　　　　folded in the bow of his birch bark canoe

　　　　　When the dream floundered
　　　　　in a cold sea
　　　　　he donned the robe himself
　　　　　to play White God

for the Indians
At Green Bay, Michigan

MAN 2   Caron, Garnier, Vignal, Jogues,
Lalement and Brébeuf

TOGETHER Our Father which art in heaven
Grant us the strength to carry thy fiery cross
From heathen stake to heathen stake — Amen

MAN 1   Up Main Street — the Mighty Ottawa —
portage, portage
around the Chaudière Falls, Rapides Deschênes
des Chats, Chenaux, the Seven Chutes or Rocher Fendue,
Des Joachims

MAN 2   Henry Kelsey, Sir George Simpson, David Thompson,
Factor John McLean, James MacMillan, Alexander McLeod,
Norman McLeod, John McLeod, John McLouglin,
Dugald McTavish, Simon McTavish, William McTavish,
John George McTavish, William McGillvray,
Duncan McGillvray, Simon McGillvray

TOGETHER Our Father which art in heaven
Give us the shortcut to the great fur land

MAN 1   Now, turn north-west on the Mattawa
portage, portage

MAN 2   Portage des Roches,
Portage des Paresseux,
Portage de la Prairie,
Portage de la Cave,
Telon Chutes,
Portage de la Mauvaise Musique

Portage de la Tortue
La Vase . . .

INDIAN   Call me Chief Sharbot. This is my land. I belong
to it.

VOYAGEUR   Never mind him!
We must make the fort before freeze up.
Paddle for your life!

With our cargo of furs
we wintered over with the Hurons
at Témiscamingue
We forgot our beds
and our wives
We even forgot
our French names

POET   And Cadieux came in from the fur trade,
married Still Water
and settled on Calumet Island

And James Henry Raffey came in
from the Battle of Waterloo
where he was drummer boy
on Nelson's flag-ship
and settled at Renfrew

And Archibald and Annie MacKechnie
came in from Greenoch
on the *David* of London
and got their ticket for Lot Eleven,
Range Two, Ramsay Township,
Lanark County, Upper Canada

PRIEST   The voyageurs, coureurs de bois, fur-traders,
whether they are French, Scottish, English, Irish,
are completely lawless. And their debauchery is
accepted by everyone. I heard from another Jesuit
that one time the Governor of the Hudson Bay
Company arrived at Moose Factory greatly in need
of a good Indian Guide. He talked to the Hudson
Bay factor about it and the factor lined the Indian
guides up in front of the Governor and the
Governor said, "Well, which is your best Indian
Guide?" and the factor pointed to one giant blue-
eyed Indian and said, "You, MacMillan, step
forward here."

MAN I   When the pagan gods of Ireland
the Tuath-de-Dana
robbed of worship and offerings,
in the popular imagination
grew smaller and smaller
until they turned into the fairies,
the pagan heroes
grew bigger and bigger
until they turned into giants.

PRIEST   It was in the 1810s that the British Navy cut its
first timbers in the Ottawa Valley and when they
went into Ireland to impress all the slave labour to
work on the timber they took all the big Irishmen.
They took all the big ones because they could stand
up to the terrible climate, and the hard, hard work
and the cold, cold shanties in the bush. They knew
all the little Irishmen would up and die from the
cold. Oh, it was a terrible thing when the British
navymen came to take all the Big Irishmen out of
Ireland. But they knew they had to go because

if they didn't there was the Hanging Hill — and
that's why you get all these big Irishmen in the
Ottawa Valley, six foot at least, the Rafters and the
Hogans and the Mulvihills and there's the Tierneys
— and then there's all my family — the
Harringtons — even today in the old castles in
Ireland they sing a song about "the cold cold
shanties of the Ottawa Valley."

Music   "The cold cold shanties . . . "

FUR-TRADER   Good winter to you, now. Name's Donald McLean.
Been with the Hudson Bay Company since I was
14. Had some long treks in my time but I believe
my longest was on snowshoe down from James Bay
to Hull, Quebec.

It was late August, 1812 when we got our
supplies to Moose Factory but on the way out our
ship got jammed in the ice and we lost her. I felt
honour bound to reach Montreal to report the loss
to the owners. Most of my crew elected to winter
over at Moose Factory but 12 set out with me on
our little 1,200 mile hike down the Abitibi to the
headwaters of the Ottawa, on Lake Temiskaming
and then via the Ottawa River to Montreal. Late
November just before reaching Lake Temiskaming,
all but three of the crew decided to head back to
Moose Factory. I heard later two of them had died
of the cold and the others wintered over with the
Indians.

Down on the Ottawa, end of February,
snowshoeing a broad expanse of river I spotted
some children playing shinny on the ice. McCargo,
Cameron and Stranger were still with me and I said
to them, "Those must be Indian children up ahead.

But perhaps they can help us anyhow." But when we got up close to the children we near fell to our knees. They were white!

"Who are you?" I asked them.

"We are the Merrifields." they replied.

"Where are we?" I asked them.

"This is Lake Deschênes," they answered.

"Where do you live?" I asked them.

"Eardley, The Eardley Flats," they replied.

A few days later the four of us staggered around the Chaudière Portage and into Philemon Wright's Le Pigeoner in Hull. Wright fed us and sheltered us and then he drove us by sleigh all the way to Montreal.

SECTION 2 *Timber*

MAN 1   Alexander MacDonnell, the Hamiltons of
Hawkesbury, George Usborne, Peter White, Daniel
McLachlin, John Egan, George Bryson, James
Gillies, J.R. Booth.

TOGETHER   Our Father which art in heaven
Grant us our fast fortunes in white pine

CHIEF SHARBOT   Call me Chief Sharbot. This is my land. I belong to
it. When Alexander MacDonnell came to me with
that Hudson Bay man there from Golden Lake he
asked me to make treaty with him for my lands. At
first I thought MacDonnell want the beaver and I
say no to him. But the Hudson Bay man tell me he
only want the trees. So I say yes. MacDonnell signs
treaty for all the land between the Indian,
Bonnechere, Madawaska and Mississippi Rivers.
He is called the King of the Four Rivers.

TIMBER BARON   I had no intention of settling and trying to clear
PETER WHITE   the land. I knew from the beginning the money was
in lumber. I came out in 1813 with the Mercantile
Marine during the War of 1812. As soon as that
was over I got a partner and went into the
lumbering in the Lower Ottawa Valley. We began
well. Then in 1827 he disappeared from Quebec
city with all the money from the sale of that year's
lumber, leaving me to pay the company debts.
    I had heard stories of George Usborne of
Quebec City beginning again at Portage-du-Fort
and of George Bryson going up from Lanark to Fort

59

Coulonge so I decided to begin anew up river. I
took my wife, Emma and our two children to
Aylmer, Quebec, left them safely there while I
scouted for timber stands. In the winter of 1827-28
I walked from Aylmer to Pembroke and back again,
and then from Aylmer to Maitland near Brockville
to sign papers and back again, and then from
Aylmer to Pembroke and back again, a total of
some 600 miles. Finally in the spring of 1828 I put
Emma — she was pregnant again — and our two
children and all our belongings and supplies into a
canoe. Emma had heard that the Indians made
offerings to the river gods at every portage — she
cast precious family heirlooms — she didn't care —
into the Ottawa to ensure our safe journey. On
June 5, 1828, I felled the first tree on the site of
Pembroke. "This is my land. It belongs to me!"
Like sheep through a hole in the fence, hot to
make their fortunes in lumber, they came after me,
the Dunlops, the Supples, the O'Kellys, the
O'Mearas, the Moffats, the Bells, the Hales, the
MacKays, the Heenans, the Frasers, the Pinks, the
Edwards, the Murrays, the Mackies — the
Shannons.

Music   Scottish Hymn

SETTLER'S WIFE   Eighty-four pilgrims
shedding a ravaged past
at Montreal our journey on foot
to McNab Township was begun,
following a tortuous trail
through tall timbers
such as our eyes could not believe,

such as frightened the children's dreams
by night.
From Lachine we huddled together
on an open barge
until our landing at Pointe Fortune

The government had contracted
a young man by the name
of Daniel McLachlin
of Arnprior
to transport our goods,
and the women and children —
yes, three oxen pulling Indian travois
for eighty-four people,
some pregnant,
some with babes-in-arms,
some sick with fevers . . .
and then through forest and swamp again,
suffering the June swarms of black flies
and mosquitoes, not even knowing enough
to build a smudge at dark;
for eleven days to Hawkesbury
where we stood for a gentle moment
and looked upon cleared fields,
log buildings, lands already claimed,
a sprouting of early crops . . .
and then onwards with Scottish hymns
in tears and Gaelic sung,
for two more days
and terrible nights
to Aylmer, Quebec,
where we boarded a steamer,
the old *Union*,
and went up the Ottawa River

to where Arnprior stands today
the Indians and the animals
came out of the forest
to look at us

mutations
crawled up out of the ocean.

PRIEST   In 1785 Daddy Tom Hodgins
was born in Tipperary
and in 1823 Daddy Tom helped
with the survey of Clarendon Township,
Pontiac County, Lower Canada
and chose for himself Lot Number Eleven
on the Sixth Range
He immediately married
Thankful Alfreda Kelly of Pontiac Village
and produced fourteen Protestants
for purgatory . . .

JOHN MCINTYRE   We arrived at the Arnprior steamboat landing June
1825 and met together at the Laird's Kennel Lodge.
His henchman read off the names —

JANET MCINTYRE   He told us McNab Township had been given to
him because he was the Highland Chief. We could
locate where we wanted. He would give us location
tickets later. It must have been instinct of some
kind but John, his brother Donald and his father
Peter, all the McIntyres headed seven miles up the
Madawaska to the Flat Rapids — as far away from
McNab as we could get then —

JOHN   Very early in the game we learned we had leant up on a reed. McNab had promised us three months' provisions upon arrival out of Mr. Ferguson's store at the mouth of the Madawaska. But when I walked the seven miles in, all that was in Mr. Ferguson's fine store was a large puncheon of whiskey —

JANET   An Indian neighbour, Mrs. Buckshot, showed us how to make tea out of the birchbark. We were able to get some seed for the following spring and John cleared more land.

JOHN   Then in November I heard that Alexander MacDonnell of Sand Point was hiring men to go into his lumber camps for the winter and bring out the white pine. Janet, it's a dollar a day! I'm going!

JANET   Ach, you foolish man! MacDonnell's a friend of McNabs. You'll never get paid.

JOHN   I'll buy you a shawl of Chinese silk.

JANET   Well, he went and me expecting. God Almighty! Some land agent back in Dockhart told us the snow is not deep enough in Canada to obstruct road travel! After one storm — when John was away in the lumbercamp — it took me two days to shovel out of the shanty. I met my neighbours, the Donald McIntyre's shovelling in! We met in a tunnel! — and the loneliness — 'tis akin to starvation — some women went mad with loneliness, keeping the fires burning, trying to care for small children — But I was too busy to go mad with loneliness — my family sent me wool from Scotland — all winter long I knit in tune with the wind —

LADY SIMPSON   Oh, they all said he was too old for me and of
course, he was! But he promised me he would settle
down. And at his age, I thought he would. I
thought I'd have my fill of adventure in the wilds of
Canada and then he would retire from the Hudson
Bay and we could go back to England and enjoy
civilization and all that money. But not George
Simpson! And the honeymoon! Oh, it was a rare
one! From Lachine to Hudson's Bay, me, George
and ten Indian and voyageur paddlers — and me
fresh from Miss Greshman's School for Girls in
England — shooting the rapids in a thirty-five foot
birch bark canoe — sleeping on the ground, eating
half-cooked beaver, watching the Indians devour
even the eyes of the fish — no, as it turned out, not
even an eighteen-year-old bride could keep
Governor George Simpson at home! Oh everytime
I'd see that Highland piper getting ready I'd know
they were off again — I got to hate that piper!

POET   When I see you again

after the long cruel feudal
dominion of the wintertime
when I see you again
it will be like
standing
in a hush of cedars

first,
you will put your hand
on my head

holy, holy, holy

and then we will
astonish
the spring

MAN 2　For forty days and forty nights
we blew in the Atlantic winds,
Canaanites by compass
to the promised land,
herded into the hold like cattle,
living and hoping
amongst the sick and dying;
we had a stowaway on board,
the young widow, Mary Kilmartin;
back in dear Ireland
when the potatoes turned black
she had murdered her three children
rather than listen to them
slowly starving to death;
we hid her
and fed her our nothings.

Music　"Oh, fare thee well, sweet Donegal . . ."

POET　From Kilkee in County Clare
bride and groom
we came to the wild country

Tom Corrigan was a man who pleased me well
and I was pleased to give him a son,
first child born in the wilderness

we were like Adam and Eve
at the beginning of Time

We had no one to tell
the joyous news

So we carried
him out into the clearing
down by the river's sound
and we walked around
and held him up
so God could see him

our love-child
our first-born

a holy child

first child in the wilderness

FANNIE CORRIGAN I hate to admit it but I think maybe the Morriaritys
and the Kinnellys were in here before us on the
Opeongo — they say they came in the back door
by Peterson Line and in to Mount St. Patrick. But
Tom and I were here alone at first and then he was
out hunting one day and he saw another man's
tracks in the bush and he followed the track right
into the Morriarity place — and he found there
was somebody else in the Opeongo Country —
besides himself — and me. Well, you can imagine
how he felt! And we got together — the Mick
Kinnellys and Morriaritys and the Orange
Corrigans. And we've been friends ever since.
And then the Heinzes came here. They came from
Germany down through Sebastapol and they drove
a herd of sheep through the bush and they didn't
know anybody else was here at all. And there were

two Kinnellys on two farms by that time and they
heard sheep baaing in the bush and they knew
somebody else must be in. And they told us and we
all went down together and met Mr. Heinz. And he
was pure German out from Germany and he
couldn't speak a work of English but we all became
friends and neighbours anyhow and worked
together from then on. And old Mr. Heinz, until
the day he died spoke English with an Irish accent
because he learned it all from the Kinnellys,
Moriartys, and Corrigans. All the German people
around here have an Irish accent and a lot of the
French riverdrivers who married Irish girls and
settled here, learned bits and pieces of English that
comes out pure Irish.

TOM CORRIGAN   It is not easy to make a new place in the wilderness
here with only an axe. But with starvation at your
back you do it. I have learned ten new things about
stones and the joints of my back and I have become
ten new men. I am not a wholly unbelievable
investment of man-pride. I am the overlord of one
hundred acres of Opeongo Line, its total perimeters
not yet seen by me or any of mine. My kin are
starving on a half acre of land in County Armagh
but I am afraid to write of the news of this land for
the taking — yes, in case they all, like drowning
rats, desert the ship of Hugh O'Neil and come out
here — and there would be no land left for my
children's children — I mean, I do not know how
far this land reaches or how much of it remains to
be given out — there must be an end to it — every
land must have a Land's End — they tell me it goes
from ocean to ocean — but how can they know

67

that? — for surely no one man in his whole lifetime
travels could cover such extraordinary distances —
unless he were to sprout wings — and fly like a
bird.

POET   Listen!

In every night of the world
home is love's long-standing relationship
to wind

in the first dawning of the New Land
he, mated male
outside
he built it

as proof of promise

inside,
she lined it

sometimes singing

and home is a place where
when they know somebody is coming
by night
they always put a light
in the window.

ANTOINETTE   When I married Fightin' Joe Godin, he was some
GERVAIS GODIN   catch for a husband — muscles, bronze, slim, ready
for anything — not the thing you see now —
balding, bleary-eyed, with a paunch on him that
would do service on a Montreal priest. He began

with the Hudson Bay Company as just a plain voyageur who could not read or write. But he was as strong and quick as Joe Montferrand and the company moved him up, even sent him to the post as Lake Témiskamingue, one of their most dangerous posts because the Indians had been cheated and tricked for so long they had learned to cheat and trick —

When I fell in love with Joe Godin he was factor at Fort Coulonge. My mother said, "Ah, Antoinette Gervais, you'll rue the day. They are all the same. A mistress in every fort." But who listens to her mother when she has met a man whose very touch turns her inside out?

Fightin' Joe Godin! Some catch he was then for a blacksmith's daughter from Fort Coulonge — there in the bush? Joe taught himself to read and write during the winters at Fort Coulonge. He wrote me letters every week he was away and he came to visit often when the weather was good — and then last week I got this letter from him. It said, "Dear Lucille, I will be in Montreal by June 24 and will kiss you behind the ears the moment I arrive. I am bringing with me the ten prime otter skins you asked for me to keep your little gambarouche warm."

Well, better he had never learned to write. A mistress in Montreal he had! I went straight to Mr. Thane the Hudson Bay District head here in Montreal. I'd fix that Fightin' Joe Godin!
But Mr. Thane read the letter and then rose up and said, "Begone vile woman! How dare you bring me such a letter! How dare you betray a good Hudson Bay man!

MAN I One time the strongest man in Ontario went over the river to find the strongest man in Quebec? After he had gone a little ways, he met a man pulling stumps out of a field with his bare hands.

"Excusez-mois, but are you the strongest man in Quebec?" he asked.

"No," answered the man stumping the field with his bare hands, "He's a little ways up the road."

The strongest man in Ontario went a little further and he met another man ploughing with two ploughs, one in each hand.

"Excusez-moi" said the strongest man in Ontario, "but are you the strongest man in Quebec?"

"No" said the ploughman, "He's a little ways up the road there."

The strongest man in Ontario went a little further until he met a very large man sitting on a very large stump sharpening a very large broadaxe.

"Excusez-moi," said the strong man from Ontario,"but are YOU the strongest man in Quebec?"

"Yes, I think so," said the big man, catching himself by the back of the coat collar and turning himself upside down with one hand, and then turning himself back into a sitting position on the stump. Then the big man stood up with his head in the trees, put his enormous broadaxe on his shoulder, did a little stepdance and sang out,

"I am big Joe Montferrand
No man on the Ottawa
Can stand up to big Joe Montferrand."

FANNIE CORRIGAN   And the strongest man in Ontario said, "I guess so!" And he ran down to Quyon on the double and caught the ferry to Fitzroy Harbour.

I heard it from an aunt in Bytown who heard it from a cousin in Montreal that there used to be a society of Roman Catholic gossips in Quebec. It was women and girls who were supposed to meet every week and report on each other, tell every good and evil deed they knew about every person they knew.

JANET MCINTYRE   I can hardly believe that.

FANNIE   Well, you'd better believe it! And then all that information went to the priests who could arrange punishments — and the excommunications.

JANET   Imagine!

FANNIE   And they said that a certain noble French lady had her hand withered by the priests because she dressed her niece in a low-necked dress — and curled her hair —

JANET   Now, that's terrible hard to believe.

FANNIE   So you find that hard to believe! Have you ever been to Rockingham?

JANET   Well, I heard there was nobility at Rockingham — but I never heard the whole story.

FANNIE   Oh! The Rockingham castle was built in England by William the Conqueror — and it's still there they say — and the young Marquis — his everyday name is John Watson — and back there in Merrie Olde England he fell in love with Mary Maroney, the gate-keeper's daughter. And when he up and married her his father banished them both to Canada — but before they sailed he relented a little — he gave them 65,000 pounds to start.

JANET   And I came with nothing!

FANNIE   John and Mary collected a gang of servants — they say they even brought a vet — and they went in to 1,000 acres on Rockingham Creek and they built everything right off — church, school, blacksmith's shop, houses — things it is taking us centuries to get —

JANET   Have you ever seen Rockingham?

FANNIE   Good God no! That's over 20 miles away! But I saw him once.

JANET   Yes —

FANNIE   He was riding his fine horse right up the Opeongo Line and he was wearing his black top hat — they say he always wears it riding.

JANET   And how are they doing, John and Mary?

FANNIE   Oh, I hear down the line they are living unhappily ever afterwards. They say he always eats alone. Mary has to wait on him in the dining room and then she and the children eat in the kitchen — they say they don't speak.

POET Love, for the free and married well
is a tiny fragile flame
you hold in your hand

You may fan it
or you may blow it out

Every day you get up
you make that choice,
both of you

FANNIE Oh, Janet, my girl, did you hear it?

JANET Hear what?

FANNIE That old Widow Kinnelly — a terror she is — was
in seeing Doc Connell at Mount St. Patrick the
other day and he was explaining to her how if you
are blind in one eye you are always sure to get
stronger in the other, and if you're deaf in one ear,
you're always sure to get stronger in the other. And
do you know what she said to him?

JANET Speak.

FANNIE She said, "Sure, by God, I have often noticed too,
if a man was short on one leg, he was always sure to
be longer on the other."

JANET Is it true she was in on the bank robbery at Renfrew?

FANNIE Oh, to be sure. She was in the bank there counting
up poor old Paddy Kinnelly's hard-earned money
he left her when the robbers came and made
everybody lie down side by side tied up on the

73

floor. And somebody said to her afterwards, "Oh, my, Mrs. Kinnelly! That must have been a terrible ordeal for you!" And she said, "Oh, not at all. That's the first time in my life I ever lay down between two good men."

JANET   Which reminds me of a good story — if you can shut up for a minute —

FANNIE   I'm all ears —

JANET   This nun went into the maternity ward in the Catholic hospital in Pembroke and she walked up to one of the patients and said:
      "And how many is this for you, my child?"
      "My fourth, Sister"
      "Well, God bless you, you're a Catholic, of course?"
      "Yes, Sister."
      "Keep up the good work."
And the nun moved on to the next one and she said:
      "And what one is this for you, my child?"
      "This is my seventh child, Sister."
      "God bless you both. You're Catholic, or course?"
      "Yes, Sister."
So the nun moved on to the next patient and said:
      "How many is this for you?"
      "Eight."
      "And you're Catholic?"
      "Oh, no Sister! I'm Protestant."
So the nun went out of the room and turned to this other nun and said, "That's an old horny bitch, that one, isn't she?"

UPPER-CLASS LADY It was fashionable, you know, for royalty and noblemen from England to visit the colonies and tour the Ottawa Valley. In 1872 Prince Arthur who later became the Duke of Connaught and the Governor General of Canada travelled up the Ottawa to Otter Lake with his hosts, representatives of two of the largest lumber companies in North America, the Gillies Brothers and the Gilmour Brothers.

One of the highlights of the Duke's trip was a hunting expedition up the Picanoc River. Some of the Gillies and Gilmour French-Canadian shantymen accompanied the royal party to make the fires, cook the meals, act as guides. According to their legend, the Prince was a magical hunter; one time when he aimed at a black duck he shot a white one. The French-Canadian shantymen were so amused by the Prince's attempts at hunting in Canada that they made up a song about it.

Music "*V'la le bon vent . . .* "

MAN 2 When Edward, the Prince of Wales
and his too too titled entourage
were roistering up the Grand River
on the Grand Tour of 1860
word went ahead
that his high high highness
had decided
to make an unscheduled stop
off the Ann Scissons
to stay at Granny Quilty's
stopping-place in Quyon.

a horrified Granny Quilty
rose to the occasion —
china from the Egans,
silver from the Bronsons,
crystal from the Mohrs,
damask from the Dahms.

yes, everything!
including a Limoges pee-poet
in the forever popular pattern
called Shamrock and Rose

borrowed from the Shady Lady
from Luskville.

FATHER
HARRINGTON

In 1850 my great-uncle on my grandmother's side
Joe Leplaunt came in from the Ottawa River
at Farrell's Landing and walked up the Opeongo Line
until he couldn't put one foot ahead of the other

and stopped and built Plaunt's Hotel

they say he built it of black ash
because black ash never burns

It never did.

HOTEL-KEEPER

Well, word just come through. He got away to
the States.

SHANTYMAN

Who?

KEEPER PUSSY

Paddy Peterson from the Peterson Line there — the one
that shot Scotty The Man Mayhew at Murphy's hotel in
Calabogie the other night.

SHANTYMAN Well, if they can get them up to Rogue's Harbour fast enough and get them saddled up with a good horse, they can almost always get them out.

RIVERMAN Calabogie is a wild place. It always was. I've had my fights from Arnprior to Sudbury but Calabogie is the damnest place for fights that ever was.

SHANTYMAN I've gone in for Gillies and Gilmour, even for Egan. If there's one thing this valley has produced its real fightin' men.

RIVERMAN I've run against the Brennans of Pontiac county — and the Stewarts of Braeside —

SHANTYMAN I have known of fellows that would take a dislike of each other for good. Take the Klosses and the Lalondes back there at Shute and Quadeville. They fought every time they met on the road. You could class it as a feud.

RIVERMAN And that was a terrible fight at Dacre when Rory MacDonald had his eyes gouged out. Men talked about that. Men still talk about that.

SHANTYMAN I heard he was asking for it.

RIVERMAN You've heard about young Conway back of Renfrew there —

SHANTYMAN The Pollacks killed him with an axe.

RIVERMAN No, a tomahawk. I heard all about that story from my grandfather McNulty that ran Rogue's Harbour.

He and a bunch went in to see Young Conway the next day. He was still living. I remember my grandfather saying that when he was breathing the blood would pump out his neck. They used a tomahawk, you know.

SHANTYMAN   I heard he was asking for it.

RIVERMAN   That's not all what happened at all. He crashed this Polish wedding with two Mulvihills and a McGee. And right off, one of the Mulvihills — it only takes them a couple of seconds for those ones to start a fight — got into it with one of the Polish wedding guests. And the rest of the Poles went in to help them and by god! his chums run away — and he got it!

SHANTYMAN   The Irish and Poles never got along — too much alike.

RIVERMAN   That was the worst day Calabogie ever saw. My grandfather McNulty said that the Irish was walking up and down the streets, gathering, arming with anything and everything. There was going to be a Polish massacre. The women were down on their knees praying and Father Harrington was running from man to man, talking them down — they closed the five bars — I guess that helped a bit.

SHANTYMAN   Ever heard of Shanty Jack Gilchrist from Pembroke?

RIVERMAN   Worked with him one winter up on the Coulonge for Gillies — he could spit the biggest tobacco spit I ever saw a man spit —

SHANTYMAN   Well this is a story about Shanty Jack Gilchrist up
            on the Pickanock for Gillies. There was no liquor
            in the lumbercamps but particularly in the Gillies
            camps. They were teetotallers and dead against
            liquor for anybody else either. Well Shanty Jack
            was up there the very winter when Gillies had just
            banned butter in all his camps as well — it was too
            expensive — and the men were really angry about
            this. It was the last straw. So Shanty Jack was
            standing right by the door when Gillies came in to
            inspect the camp. "Do I smell whiskey here?"
            Gillies roared out. "Well" snapped Shanty Jack,
            "you sure as hell don't smell butter."

Music   "Chapeau Boys"

KEEPER   Running a stopping-place in this country is sure
            getting to be a dangerous business.

SHANTYMAN   What now, Marie-Louise?

KEEPER   Why haven't you heard about the terrible thing
            that happened at Annis Norlock's the other night
            in Wilno —

SHANTYMAN   No —

KEEPER   Sure, she was killed in her own place with a sleigh-
            stake. Trying to stop a fight — the whole place was
            into it and they were tearing it up — and she went
            in to save it all.

SHANTYMAN   Those damn Poles will use those sleigh-stakes.

KEEPER   I'm going to have to get a bodyguard.

SHANTYMAN   I'd guard your body — for a little . . .

KEEPER   Drink up, me lads. I'm off to the wake at Wilno. I've been to all the wakes. I've been to some great wakes. I've been to wakes that went on for weeks with the body going to worms in the far-away barn — but the greatest was that one over back of the Bufferaw Road —

SHANTYMAN   What one was that, Marie-Louise?

KEEPER   Well, you remember when those Brannigan boys robbed the bank in Montreal and shot the three policemen . . . ?

SHANTYMAN   I heard they hid out in the Pontiac bush here for considerable time.

SHANTYMAN   And then they hung them in Montreal.

KEEPER   And then they brought the three of them back to Bufferaw for waking — and I was right there standing by the three coffins when the relative come in from Detroit or Chicago — and he come late and they hadn't had time to tell him the circumstances — or they were afraid to maybe — and I was standing right there when he said it —

SHANTYMAN   Said what, for god's sakes?

KEEPER   He looked down at them and said, "My, my Mrs. Brannigan the undertaker has done a fine job — but why are their necks so long?"

SHANTYMAN   Give me another drink.

KEEPER   Yes, drink up, me lads.

SHANTYMAN   Were you around a few years ago when Larry Frost
escaped the constables — he swam down the
Petawawa River and across the Ottawa to the
Quebec side —

RIVERMAN   I heard about that. I think Larry Frost is the
greatest — he killed a man back there on the
Petawawa.

SHANTYMAN   Yep, back in a Booth camp. And the constables
were taking him by canoe to prison in Pembroke
and he just jumped ship and swam away — hid in
Pontiac County in the bush there.

RIVERMAN   I heard he was back the very next winter up the
Black River, foreman for Gillies —

RIVERMAN   Yes, those big lumberman are always looking for
cheaper ways to get their timbers to market — one
time one of them used Oiseau Rock . . .

SHANTYMAN   I think that was Gillies.

RIVERMAN   Yes, I think that was Gillies. He was cutting timber
around Oiseau Rock that winter and he decided to
shoot them off in the spring. He thought they'd get
a headstart downriver.

SHANTYMAN   I heard the plan overworked.

RIVERMAN   That's right. They caught fire in mid-air and were
all charred. Charred before they ever hit the
Ottawa . . .

SHANTYMAN   Larry Frost is — was the greatest.

RIVERMAN   He can't touch Joseph Montferrand

SHANTYMAN   Larry was a Goliath — I heard one time —

RIVERMAN   Did you ever hear about Joe Montferrand and the Battle of the Chaudière Bridge.

SHANTYMAN   No

RIVERMAN   I thought everybody had heard that story . . . Well, one time Big Joe Montferrand was on one of his spring sprees in Bytown and he went to cross the Chaudière to Hull where he had a girlfriend by the name of Cécile Courvall. Now the Shiners were always after Joe Montferrand. They were always trying to run the French-Canadians out of the lumbercamps and take their jobs and Joe, well, Joe was the champion of the Frenchmen — as this time the Shiners got wind that Joe was going to be crossing the foot-bridge to Hull — and they gathered up a gang to waylay him — and get rid of him — for good.

    At first Joe held them off — you know with Montferrand it wasn't just that he was so big and strong but he was so quick — and he could use his feet just as well as he could use his fists — but even Montferrand couldn't hold off a dozen or so men and he could see they were getting the best of him. So he just grabbed the smallest of them — a little Irishman by the name of Dirty Dan Hickey and he held the little Irishman by one leg and used him as a flail to beat off all the others.

And ever after that Dirty Dan Hickey — I seen it for myself — had one leg stretched eight inches longer than the other —

Music   Fiddle

WOMEN   Oh, how we loved to dance with Big Joe Montferrand!

WOMAN 1   He could swing us up to the rafters.

WOMAN 2   He could swing us until our hair went straight and our head went dizzy.

WOMAN 1   The only trouble was that it took two days for the curl to come back into our hair.

WOMAN 2   The only trouble was that it took two days for our heads to clear.

POET   I come to you
like wildflowers

you gather me in
like old hayfields

all Valley dancers
have the grace
of grass

SHANTYMAN   Name's Jim Doherty. I'm the Lad from Ragged Chute at Quyon, Quebec. I've worked all my life in the lumbercamps all through the Valley. Everybody knows me. Well, one time I was walking this bunch

of greenhorns into a Booth lumbercamp in the
Upper Pontiac. Jesus Christ! What a motley crew!
Farmers from Almonte and Glengarry, young boys
of fourteen going in for the first time, old
shantymen who couldn't keep up —

Well, they were walking in but they didn't know
how far it was. It was supposed to be ten miles. We
walked quite a piece and met a lad coming out.

"How far to the camp"

"Oh, about ten miles," he says.

So we walked on another piece quite a ways further
and we met another lad.

"How far is it to the Booth camp?"

"Oh, about ten miles," he says.

So we walked a bit further and the same thing
happened again. They were getting fed up,
grumbling, tired, hungry. So I turned to them and
yelled, "Come on, you crippled bastards! Step
along! Can't you see we're holding our own!"

RIVERMAN   "The drive is on!"
and down they come,
Big Bob Connolly
of the Clarendon Front,
Martin Hennessy
of Fort Coulonge,
Black Pat Ryan
of Pontiac Village,
Mountain Jack Thompson
of Portage-du-Fort,
Gentleman Paddy Dillon,
King of the Madawaska

Listen!
Coming down around
Calumet Island at night,
the giant rivermen,
Quebec-bound,
Singing Bobalong-Donda . . .

Music   "The Rafting Song"

SHANTYMAN   Some of the best days of my life were when I was a
young man in the woods working for Egan and
Gilmour. I was born to the woods. My grandfather
and my father were slide masters at the Mountain
Chute Slide. Every morning at daylight from May
to August when the drive was on my father had to
cross the river and open the entrance boom to the
slides. When the timber was running we could look
up a mile and a quarter and see cribs coming down
the Ottawa over D'Argis Rapids. Sometimes the
force of the water would twist the cribs a little and
then we'd see a man with a ledge hammering in a
wooden pin. We'd see him do this and then in
about so many seconds we would hear the echo of
the hammering coming down the Ottawa for a
mile. Many's a time we got on one of those cribs
and shot through our slides and continued our joy
ride right down to Portage-du-Fort, over the D'argis
Rapids, around Devil's Elbow, over the Cascade at
Portage — four wonderful miles by water.

Music   Fiddle

RIVERMAN   Moses Lamuir, an Algonquin Chief, was one of the
greatest fiddlers this country ever saw. And God!

They were good rivermen! So light on their feet!
So agile! And they'd leave the camp every
Saturday night and go home in this big pointer up
the river, and one would play the fiddle and the
rest of them rowed. Say, you never heard music like
it in your life! Coming off that water. Not a sound.
Except the music. And the loons for miles around
would be hollering. You'd hear loons where there
had never been loons before. And they could ALL
play the fiddle. And the mouth organ. And the
Jew's Harp. And it was good music. Where they
learned it, I don't know. Nor how.

Music   Fiddle

UPPER-CLASS LADY   Pembroke was always gay. There was all that
money and then there was the Petawawa military.
It was endles parties and military euchres and balls
and picnics and cruises down the Ottawa River.
　　One of the most vivid memories of my
childhood in Pembroke was standing at my own
gate one clear bright January day and watching
Delia Shannon go by. She was one of the
lumbering Shannons and she married a Mackie,
another one of the big lumbering families in town.
Delia was beautiful — black, black hair and lovely
brown eyes — and she was dressed entirely in white
fox, white fox coat and hat, even muff, I think. She
was in a red sleigh with musk-ox robes around her
feet. It was a single-horse sleigh and the horse wore
silver harness with troika bells. The driver had a
black bearskin cape over his shoulders. She must
have been going to an afternoon party. She waved.

POET Upon my love
I do so think of you
when the wind blows
and the sun shines
and the rain falls

Upon my love
I do so think of you
when winter snows
and spring flowers
and summer ripens

Upon my love
I do so think of you
at every heart-beat
of the universe

Upon my love
I do so think of you
when the wind blows
and the sun shines
and the rain falls

CHIEF SHARBOT I, Chief Sharbot
of the Sharbot Lake Reserve
a few years ago I saw
the timber barons,
Gillies, MacLachlin,
Edwards and Booth
standing on the bridge
at Radiant Lake,
watching their barkmarked logs
go through the timber slide,
silently tallying their riches,

making small talk
to hide the secrets
white men of power
keep to themselves.

SECTION 3 *Tom Murray*

TOM MURRAY Name's Tom Murray. I was born in 1880 on the Opeongo Line — second generation. My mother told me how the shantyman used to walk up the Opeongo Line to go to work for McLaughlin or Barnett or Booth. She told me about this great bit Scotsman named MacGillvray. He weighed over three hundred pounds and he was walking by her door and he stopped and asked for water. My mother brought him a dipperful. But he said to her "Good God, my girl! That's no good to me! Bring me the pail!" My mother couldn't write her name but she was one of the smartest women on earth.

And my father would be sitting at the table reading the *Montreal Weekly Star* — that was his bible. I can remember him reading to us about Louis Riel. And we'd listen to him at the big long table with a candle at each end. We were slow in getting the coal oil.

I can tell you a great story about the Opeongo Line. There was a school teacher named Gibson teaching in there at Madawska near the Egan Estates. He went to Barry's Bay in the winter of 1869, drank some bad liquor and died. The trustees found a replacement in John Wesley Dafoe, one of the greatest men his country ever produced — in my opinion. Dafoe came from Combermere by birch bark canoe and landed in at MacLachlin's Depot in Barry's Bay and joined some other shantymen who were walking in to the Madawaska. One of the uneducated shantyman was John Hunt, the blacksmith from Mount St. Patrick.

John was a great blacksmith but he hadn't had
much schooling and it was always said afterwards
that the only formal education of any kind John
Hunt ever had was that long, long walk to
Madawaska with John Wesley Dafoe!

PRIEST   On Dominion Day, 1867,
Daddy Tom Hodgins died at home in Shawville
having managed to see the whole Ottawa Valley
with an army of Orangemen for purgatory —
Dales, Wilsons, MacDowells, Lawtons,
Clarks, Andersons, Daggs, McFalls, Judds,
Kellys, Webbs, Horners, Baileys, Balharries,
Workmans, Browns, Johnstons, Dahms,
Millers, Tweedles, Murrays, Pauls,
Dodds, McQueens, McLeans.

POET   When we were cradled in the Valley
always a river ran through
the fingers of our childhood
and fed our spirit-mouths
so that we grew up
entirely in ignorance
of thirst

in those beginning times
who knew about the steady
hypnotic promises
of the westward plains
and the prairie
granaries?

the Valley was the whole world
the River ran through all of us
and enclosed us.

PRIEST   The last raft of square timber went down the
         Ottawa in 1911 for J.R. Booth. The Indian who
         made the treaty with Alexander MacDonnell for
         the timber stands at the Indian, Mississippi,
         Madawaska and Bonnechere Rivers thought the
         timber would never end. But it did. And the great
         Depression started creeping inland. From the
         Ottawa Valley the exodus of the young people
         began, looking for work to the mines of the north,
         to the granaries of the west, to the car plants of
         Detroit. So well I remember, in a sermon at Mount
         St. Patrick, Father Dowdall sounding out, almost in
         tears,
         "They are going, going, gone
         And we cannot bid them stay."

POET   When he was young, slim, tall
         in the saddle, his green eyes full
         of the girls watching him, he rode
         in the Calgary Stampede with Tom
         Three Persons, learned he could
         not ride with the Indians. Later
         in the Shining Tree Country
         a vanishing tribe taught him
         everything they knew about
         keeping warm, finding direction,
         righting a canoe, single-handed.
         I lie beside him in his ancestral
         house imagining the woodland God
         he once was, wishing I had been
         a ripe young bitch in Sudbury
         when he came out of the headwaters
         of the Ivanhoe after six months
         on the diamond-drills, his manhood
         drowned in company doses of salt-
         petre, waiting with hard nipples

and an ache between my legs
for the bright dancing horses
of his desire. In restless turnings
between the snores and farts of
aging lovers when I fall asleep
beside the old stud, I dream two women,
one dark, one fair, ride from the west
and the north, bearing his children
in their arms. "Tell me," I cry out,
turning to him, "Tell me where they are
that I may go and see them once
before I die." The old rider holds me
in his arms. "So help me God! I do
not remember the trails I took,
nor the ones I left behind me —
besides, the tents and the villages
are all gone —" he kisses my eyes,
running salt-tears, and tells me
I am the only woman — after Mary —
that he has ever loved.

How can I love such a seasoned liar?
When the old ranger slips into the paddock of sleep
again, the name he calls out is Cathewana.

TOM MURRAY   Now, Father, go back to 1840 for a minute. The
Government of Upper Canada sold out all this
pine country to all the aristocrats from the Old
Country, Skeads, Conroys, Egans — people who
came with lots of money to begin with. Then the
second lot came in; J.R. Booth from Ottawa bought
the Egan Estates at Madawaska in 1867 and Dan
MacLachlin from Arnprior bought out Skead. In
1910, M.J. O'Brien from Renfrew there bought
MacLachlin's old limit on the Madawaska. They

passed around the limits, you know. At that time, the limit-holders had the water-power rights too. M.J. O'Brien had limits he bought for twenty thousand dollars and in 1929 right in the Depression — he sold the water-power rights to Ontario Hydro for one million eight thousand dollars. That's one way he made money — besides mining and railways.

Talk about Depression! I mean the First Depression in 1893. You know Tom how terrible it was in Barry's Bay. About fifty Italians were working on the railroad back in the mud in a swamp there building a grade — the foreman of that gang came into Barry's Bay every two weeks and bought everything for them. Yes. Every two weeks he bought two sheeps and two bags of potatoes.

And people don't understand the Thirties Depression, how bad it was. My brother Red Mick Murray one cold cold day last January, went down to Renfrew to visit his bank — he had some money and if you had some money you never banked in your own town because then everybody in town would know your business — and when he got back from Renfrew, I asked him, "How were things down in Renfrew today, Mick?" And he said, "Oh, terrible, Tom, terrible. There was only smoke coming out of two chimneys, M.J. O'Brien's and Father Harrington's."

SECTION 4 *The Parade*

POET It is not
so much the mountains
which keep
The Valley
warm

it is
the Valley-
people

MAN 1 Here comes King Billy on his White Horse!

MAN 2 Boysaboys! The Micks are waiting for them at the
Burnstown Inn.

MAN 1 Merciful Jesus! What a fight there'll be!
Better than the Ballygiblin Riots,
yessiree, yessiree

MAN 2 There goes Big-Mouth Mulligan

MAN 1 There goes the King of the Madawaska

PEDDLAR Come and get it!
Come get Mrs. Lolly's Love Potion!
Cures all lovers' ailments including;
hyper-acidity, frigidity,
unsatisfactory genitalia, mammalia, allalia,
nagging husbands and straying wives,
sagging mediatric sex drives,

fetishes and unexpected wetishes,
venereal diseases,
shortness of breath, night cramps and wheezes,
forgotten birthdays and incompatibility,
unisexuality and unexpected fertility,
apathy, grapathy and anything that doesn't happathy
brutishness, hirsutishness and fruitishness,
adultery, connultery, virultery

ENDORSED BY WORLD FAMOUS DOCTORS
THROUGHOUT THE WORLD!

Come and get it! Mrs. Molly's Love Potion
Fify cents a bottle!

MAN 2   There goes the Renfrew Millionaires

MAN 1   There goes the sixty-minute-men
         Moose Johnson,
         Pud Glass,
         Eagle-Eye Lehman

MAN 2   Yes, there goes the Shawville Express

MAN 1   There goes the Shady Lady of Luskville

MAN 2   There goes the Witch of Waltham
         There goes lard-ass

MAN 1   A good woman, you know, is always
         six axe-handles
         across the rear

MAN 2   For a woman like that
         he should crawl on his belly
         through glass!

MAN 1   There goes the Silver Seven

MAN 2   There goes Cy Denneny

MAN 1   There goes Punch Broadbent

MAN 2   There goes Cyclone Taylor

MAN 1   There goes Midnight Walsh

MAN 2   There goes Cadillac Bob

MAN 1   There goes Big Bird

MAN 2   There goes Four Faces

MAN 1   Here goes Dangerous Dan Tye
You have to watch that guy!

MAN 2   Holy Bejesusing Christmas Trees!
Who's that coming down the midway?

MAN 1   Oh, that's the new Girl . . . !

MAN 2   Son of a bitch! did you see that!
The New Girl!
The New Girl!

MAN 1   Oh, Twelfth of July!
hold still

MAN 2   Oh, Fairtime
come again

POET   Fair-time

        finding my larger-than-life-grandfather
        at fair-time
        standing in the valley of the giants
        holding his hand

           "you must be May's daughter
           you look so much like her"

           "how come none of those girls
           are as good-looking as their mother?"

        finding Uncle Lloyd with all his horses
        and red ribbons

        finding Uncle Joe in his Orangeman's regalia
        finding thirty-two more second cousins
        even one named Cuthbertson, Scotch Louis Cuthbertson!
        finding the pie table in the Holy Roller tents
        eating 16 pieces of pie

        fair-time

WOMAN I   I've seen some great Twelfth of July fights in my day
between the Orangemen and the Micks. But I thinks
the best fight I ever saw was in the rush end of the Old
Dey's arena in Ottawa one time when I was down
visiting my great-aunt Enid Corrigan who married a
Frenchman named Deneau — he was her third, she'd
killed two before him. The rush end was a section at
both ends of the rink where you stood all night. But that
didn't matter. You were watching the Montreal Maroons
play the Ottawa Senators and Aurel Joliet was playing.

Oh, my! That little wee Frenchman! Just absolutely gorgeous! And Jack Kilrea — he was an Orangemen first, last and forever — and he was there in the Rush End watching his son, Hec, play for the Ottawa Senators. And he'd managed to save up some whisky for the game and he'd be having a few and telling everybody around, "That's my son down there!" And somebody would answer him with a vile insult, or slanderous French and oh, my God! they would be into it! More and more people would be into it, until the whole Rush End was in a melee, and then even the one's who'd paid to get in would start coming over and the whole Dey's arena would be into it — fighting, throwing bottles, cursing, swearing, in both French and English — and finally the Ottawa Senators and the Montreal Maroons were just standing on the ice watching the performance.

MAN I   The Hodgins got in here first and they came with some money and they made more. My grandfather Hodgins opened the first car dealership in the Pontiac in Shawville — and he made more. He was soon well off enough to be able to take his wife on a trip to Atlantic City — that's where everybody who was anybody went in the Twenties — became enamoured of the Atlantic Ocean, swam out beyond her depth and was hauled up on shore, half-drowned, by some nearby swimmers.

While she was lying on the beach at Granpa's feet, someone in the crowd yelled out, "Give her artificial respiration."

"Artificial respiration be damned" Granpa yelled back, "Give her the real thing! I can afford it."

MAN 2   My third cousin, old Diamond Jim Gallagher of
         Brudenell on the Opeongo Line saved all his
         money — sometimes you know, when you get a
         tight Irishman, they are tighter than any Scot from
         Glengarry to Renfrew — and he was so tight he
         wouldn't pay five cents to see Jesus Christ pass
         through Douglas — but he saved up enough money
         and he decided he would see the Big City before he
         died. So he took the train to Toronto — Aunt
         Jessie was too arthritic to go anywhere by then —
         and he got a room at the Royal York and he was
         standing in the lobby watching the elevators go up
         and down — and he saw this little old gray-haired
         lady get onto one elevator and then he say this
         young great big blonde lady get out of another
         elevator and he said out loud in the lobby, "Oh,
         dear God, I wish I had brought my old lady and put
         her through that machine!"

WOMAN 2 John T. Waite was my great-uncle on my mother's
         side. Now John T. Waite was a very religious Holy
         Roller and a good-living man to boot. No one in
         Arnprior could ever say a word against his
         character — and still be speaking the truth. For
         many years, on and off, John T. Waite had said that
         he was prepared to show that man, by faith, could
         walk on water. Everybody kept at him constantly
         until he came to the point of desperation where he
         had to prove that man, by faith could walk on
         water. So a certain Sunday morning was set and the
         old wooden wharf at the foot of John Street down
         by Inch Buie cemetery was chosen as the site. The
         event was advertised in *The Arnprior Chronicle* for
         three weeks running and by the time the appointed

Sunday arrived the whole town of Arnprior and
the people in to church from the surrounding
countryside were gathered at the Ottawa River to
be present for a miracle.

And John T. Waite went down that Sunday
morning and walked off the end of the John Street
wharf and disappeared into the depths of the
Ottawa River.
When he emerged he simply waved to the huge
crowd of onlookers and pronounced in a loud
voice,

"As you can see, my brethren, the faith of John
T. Waite was not strong enough for him to walk on
water . . . "

MAN I   Timber Baron Hiram MacTavish of Arnprior
and his wife Constance Maria MacDonnell
lived to be well on into their nineties
they had a family burial plot
at Inch Buie right by the River
but, over the years, it had filled up
with spinster aunts, second cousins,
bachelor-born uncles who had died
without having any "Burying money,"
or who had no close folks of their own
to lie with at the end

Over the years Constance Maria
always took pity on them.
"Blood is thicker than water"
she would snort as she sniffed
her British snuff. "We can't leave
a relative out in the cold!"

But when Constance Maria was dying
(she only lasted a few months after
her husband, you know),
the family discovered there was no room
for her in the MacTavish plot

Right then and there
Constance Maria created a scandal
up and down the length
of the River Valley

"I'll be cremated!" she declared
hoisting her Parisian pince-nez
"And you will put my ashes
in Hiram's grave."

"A cremated Presbyterian!"
the remaining relatives cried.

"Unthinkable!"

"Sacreligious!"

"Nonsense!" roared Constance Maria
the their chorus of protests.
"I'll be right where I want to be —
close to Hiram's heart

and besides
it will save space
and money!"

POET   Oftentimes when it rains all day
in other countries and slicks
the autumn leaves against our
window panes, I am reminded that
we both now sleep at night
smiling, without our teeth in,
and in the mornings, still full
of good humour, accuse each other
of farting in our dreams and calling
out the names of old lovers who passed
beyond all pale of meaning years ago,
before our bellies sagged and our brows
furrowed. To the unbelievers outside
there appears to be no rhyme nor reason
to the synchronization of our
heart-beats when we lie together.
How can they know that our courage
is matched and that we are both
addicted adventurers come home
to roost in the Celtic Twilight
at the foot of the mountains in Sheen?

Round-eyed
and looking at us sideways, the young
lovers have a lingering suspicion
that we are not about to reveal
the secret of our success to anyone.
And they are right. No Comment.
Except to say, "Nobody ever told us
that, at this stage of the game,
we would still be going laughing
all the way upstairs to bed."

PRIEST   For many years afterwards
up on the Grand Calumet
Cadieux's Lament,
written in blood
on a piece of birchbark,
hung on a tree
near the place
where he fell
and it is said
in the annals of the spirit
for many years afterwards
the wolf and the nightingale
visited Cadieux's last resting-place
to pay homage
to his one-man stand;

before they were driven
from the land
it was the Algonquin
who protected the stone
that marked his grave

in the end
it was the white savages
who mutilated and destroyed
the hallowed ground.

Music   Fiddle

POET   Oh, I went up the Valley
to a place called Killaloe;
We have to travel far to learn
the things we always knew

Sean Quilty, he came up to me,
the mists of Ireland in his hair,
and all his father's fathers
for generation there

Sean Quilty asked me once to dance,
and when he asked me more,
I knew that we would dance again,
I knew we'd danced before

Sean Quilty, he came up to me,
the laughter lined his Irish face;
we had that night in Killaloe,
a meeting full of grace

Sean Quilty swung me off the floor,
and whispered in my hair,
"When you and I were younger, girl,
I wish that I'd been there"

Sean Quilty, he came up to me,
the mists of Ireland in his hair,
and all his mother's mothers
for generations there

"Can we make up for time that's lost?"
"Alas, we never can, my lad;
When you and I were younger, Sean,
we chose the ones we have"

Sean Quilty, he came up to me;
the laughter lined his Irish face;
we had that day in Killaloe
a meeting full of grace

Music   Fiddle

POET   Back in the good times
before there were "no good times left —
none at all"
up on the Grand Calumet
the Singing Gavans sang
from morning to night,
mother, father,
six sons
and six daughers,
across the ringing waters
of Chenal Culbate
from Oiseau Rock
to Bryson Chute

back in the good times
it was said that the Gavan house
had more fiddles than chairs

it was said when Bridget Gavan
shook her apron
a thousand old Irish airs
fell upon the river-shore
and the wind took them
like contraband
to the four corners
of the new land

from Kamloops to Corner Brook
you can hear the songs yet
Bridget Gavan shook
from her apron
up on the Grand Calumet

Music	Fiddle

JANET   Did you hear about what Margaret MacDonnell has gone and done?

FANNIE   Those Glengarry Scots! Nothing would surprise me!

JANET   Well, her mother is dying, they say, in Williamstown and she's just taken her youngest up in front of her — she's still nursing it — and gone on her horse through the bush — back to Glengarry — all the way through Arnprior, Bytown, Metcalfe . . .

FANNIE   Well, I always have to take my hat off to them but God! they look down their noses at the Irish! — she always used to say —

JANET   Yes, she always used to say, "The dumbest man in Kerry moved to Cork and, when he did that, the overall intelligence in both countries went up."

FANNIE   And those Glengarry Men! It always seemed to me — from the little I've seen of them, of course — that they come in only two sizes — the giants and then the little bow-legged bully bandies.

JANET   Yes, they think they have a monopoly on men in Glengarry . . .

FANNIE   That reminds me of a story I heard from those Scotch settlers in the Scotch bush around Douglas — I think it was Violet Macpherson — her people used to run Macpherson's Hotel at Burnstown before the shantymen ruined it.

JANET   I heard they dance in their spiked boots until they all went through the floor.

FANNIE   Yes, and, there's a wonderful Presbyterian minister in Douglas called Canon Quartermain. He looks after the neglected children and the poor widows and the misguided girls — that Margaret MacDonnell would have you think all that kind are Irish — so you know they were putting The Good Road through Douglas and after the Good Roads Gang had left, Canon Quartermain got word that one of the poor misguided girls in Douglas — Annie Lannigan — she was Irish, was expecting — and she was NOT married. So the Canon went to visit her.

"Tell me my child," the Canon said, "who is the father of this baby that you will be having soon?"

"I can't say, reverend," Annie replied.

"Tell me, I am going to see that he does right by you."

"I really can't say," Annie persisted.

"You must at least know his name. I have to put a name down here if I am going to help you."

"Well, Canon — to be honest with you now — I guess you'll just have to put down 'The Good Roads Gang.' "

JANET   Well, you know Margaret told me a really sad story — she almost had tears in her eyes.

FANNIE   So, it's a storyteller you're becoming . . .

JANET   Back in the wilds of Glengarry, Donald MacGillvray was courting Henrietta MacMillan, daughter of Archie Roy. MacGillvray finally got up

the courage to go speak to Roy to ask for
Henrietta's hand in marriage. The request was
flatly refused.

"You must marry Bella," Archie Roy said to
Donald MacGillvray. "She is the elder. You must
marry her." MacGillvray went away very very
angry. But on the way home walking back to
Kirkhill he got to thinking. "After all," he said to
himself, "They are sisters and they look alike.
What difference does a few years make anyhow?
Why be so particular?"

So he turned around and walked back to Archie
Roy and he said, "All right then, I'll take Bella."

And Henrietta never married.

POET   Listening to the wilderness
I learned
some birds sing to find a mate,
some birds sing
to declare their territory

but some birds
free of fear
and anxiety

sing
for joy.

CARL   Sometimes on a good week-end there'll be twenty
or thirty sifting through here, through this kitchen,
sitting around telling stories, reciting dirty ditties,
drinking beer — sometimes when the Gavans
come we have real music.

SECTION 5 *Carl's Kitchen*

LLOYD   Oh, God help an Irishman! Three thousand miles from home and a tall cool beer from anywhere else —

CARL   Wasn't it old Joe Hurty who used to always say, "Thank God there isn't an Orangeman alive above Waltham!"

LLOYD   Well, down there around Shawville in Hodgins country they always say, "Thank God there isn't a Frog or a Mick in the countryside . . . "

CARL   I do have to admit, the Orangeman of Shawville put on a good fair — I think I'll go again this year.

LLOYD   Ah, but the Chapeau Fair — that's the Fair!

CARL   My father told me about the first Chapeau Fair away back in its beginnings. Black Joe Venosse rolled a great big pumpkin down the mountain from his farm to show at Chapeau Fair. And Father Renaud brought his great big bull. At noon on the first day the bull got loose and ate the pumpkin. And that was the end of the Chapeau Fair.

LLOYD   Well, I remember not too long ago when Louis Lamarsh grew a pumpkin so big he cut a door in it and kept a cow in it all winter long.

CARL   I'll tell you a real fair story. It's about the Renfrew Fair.

LLOYD   Now I have to admit the Orangemen put on a good
          fair there — I think I'll go again this year.

CARL   A long time ago when the Renfrew Fair was on
          there was always a bunch of Irishmen came down
          the Mountain to go to the fair. This story was
          passed on to me by my father and he was ninety-
          one when he died, so it was a long time ago. In
          those early days the women used to get into it —
          no siree, it wasn't just the men that got into the
          fights — and they didn't wear silk stockings either
          — they wore the long woollen ones and they used
          to fill them up with gravel and then they used them
          as bludgeons.
          Anyway, one time at the Renfrew Fair a bunch of
          the Irish people came down the Mountain and they
          got into it with a bunch of those Scots from
          Renfrew — and when it was all over, there laid one
          of them Irishmen from the Mountain who was hit
          on the head and quite, quite dead. So they had an
          inquest and hearing — dragged on and on for
          weeks and weeks and wasn't getting anywhere at all
          because Nobody knew Anything and Everybody
          said they knew Nothing. Finally, the frustrated
          magistrate issued his decree:

          "The hearing is completed. And I have decided
          that any Irishman with a skull that thin shouldn't
          have been at the Renfrew Fair."

LLOYD   My people came from the Upper Ottawa Valley —
          Pontiac County to be exact. They were very very
          very early settlers and to give you some idea of how
          early I want to tell you a story. As you probably
          know, Samuel de Champlain came up the Ottawa

River about 1650. He and his men were in three canoes and it was coming on dusk and time to encamp for the night. So they looked up ahead on the shoreline and there they espied a log cabin with smoke coming out of the chimney. So Champlain said to his men, "Mes garçons! Regardez! Regardez! And they pulled into the Ottawa shore and they were somewhat fearful. And Samuel de Champlain, being the leader, approached the log cabin himself, his sword in one hand and his pistol in the other, his men strung out along the shore with the muskets ready. And Champlain got up near the cabin. Now inside the cabin was my great-great-great-great-great grandfather looked up and said, "Come on in, Sam!"

CARL   I ask you, now who got along in this country? The Poles fought the Irish.

LLOYD   I heard they used to fight with sleigh-stakes in Annie Norlock's Hotel in Wilno.

CARL   And the Irish hate the English.

LLOYD   And the French hate the English.

CARL   I believe in the Big City — in Ottawa — those *edjicated ignoramuses* call that racial *prayjudice.*

LLOYD   Sure it all makes me laugh — there's no more pure-blood anybody — we're all cross-bred, clouded over, MONGRELS!

CARL   Everybody looked down on the Indians.

LLOYD   "There's a little of the breed in all of us," to be sure . . .

CARL   I guess you can say us Maloneys are the only pure-bloods, pure Irish left around here . . .

LLOYD   That's because the Maloneys thought nobody was good enough for the goddamn Maloneys to marry.

CARL   I always say, "Never tie a knot with your tongue you can't undo with your teeth."

LLOYD   Baloney Maloney! You'd rather burn than marry.

CARL   There was once a timber baron from Ottawa who was so-o-oo miserable he once fed all his lumbercamps for a whole winter on ten miles of baloney.

LLOYD   All those Baloney Maloneys — too miserable to marry —

CARL   I am now going to tell you one of the best true stories ever told in this kitchen, ever told in the whole Ottawa Valley —

There was once a famous widow of Chapeau . . .

LLOYD   And you damn well know who that was!

CARL   . . . and she had been a widow for a very long time. But she had remained active. She had six boyfriends, three Orangemen from one side of the river and three Dogans from the other — none of yer racial prejudices in her bed! So finally she died. And Father Harrington knew all about her and he

decided that he would commandeer all her lovers
to be her pallbearers. Of course, they all agreed.
But it was a cold windy icy January day and some of
the pallbearers slipped when they were carrying her
down the steps of the Chapeau church. And Father
Harrington just behind the coffin, hissed out at
them. "Hold on to her, boys! You did it before and
you can damn well do it this one last time!"

LLOYD   And you damn well were one of them —

POET   Summer mornings, winter evenings,
         I remember now the rising and falling,
         the "love-work"

         In this Valley of Vision
         the early tribes came and went,
         the newly-weds searching
         for ancestral blessings,
         drunken and dishonoured poets
         chorusing "We must laugh
         and we must sing"

         In the Valley of Vision
         the early tribes came and went,
         down the mountains,
         up the rivers,
         carrying the newborn
         and their dead

         Summer mornings, winter evenings,
         I have forgotten your flesh,
         but I am always in the circle
         of your arms.

CARL   God! I remember Long Jim Shea! The day they buried poor Mrs. Morriarity in Sheen there was twenty-six fights in town. And Jim Shea sang at the wake. God! Jim Shea could sing! Long Jim Shea, he was an old man when he died, ninety-eight. An old Bachelor. And oh, could he fight! He always fought at the Chapeau Fair. He never in his whole life once came home from the Chapeau Fair without a black eye. And he had this horse Tess and he could put her up against the best of them, Pembroke, Renfrew, Shawville, Quyon, anywhere. But she'd always win. And they were always razing him about Tess. So he made up some verses and sent them back on them — I can only remember some of it now —

The Sheener's pride,
The Islander's dread
they all so wished
Old Tess was dead

Trot on her tail
throw sand in her eyes
she would still come in
to win first prize

I always say "if you trot your horses when they're young, they'll still trot at seventy-two."

LLOYD   I thought you always said "If you don't run the stallion behind the buggy, he can't service the mare."

CARL   Remember Lucy Quinn of Chapeau . . .

LLOYD   How she used to ride bareback . . .

CARL   She was the one . . .

LLOYD   She was the first Roman Catholic girl that ever danced with a Protestant in Chapeau.

CARL   Father Harrington came up and put his hand on her shoulder and told her to get off the dance floor — she was sinning in the arms of a Hodgins from Shawville.

LLOYD   And Lucy Quinn just shook his hand off her shoulder and went right on dancing.

CARL   She married that Orangeman.

LLOYD   And old Mrs. Quinn wouldn't speak to her — even on her deathbed.

POET   In the Valley
I always dwelt amongst yarners,
and liars,
and poets
who were not called "poets,"
singers whose songs
could not be rendered
in other places

Indeed, it was in the Valley
I learned
to play the fiddle
with my feet

CARL   I figure I've seen just about everything, the first threshing-machine, the first car, the first steam-engine, the first aeroplane.

LLOYD   The first atomic bomb —

CARL   And I've done everything. I've gone to the lumbercamps —

LLOYD   I only went up for McCool —

CARL   — and I've worked in the mines, and I've diamond-drilled, and I've prospected.

LLOYD   — for Precious Little

CARL   — and I've farmed and I've railroaded —

LLOYD   Jack-of-all-trades, master-of-none. I guess that's the way we all were.

CARL   And I've lived with the Indians at Témiscamique. God when those Indian girls were sixteen they'd make things stand that had no feet.

LLOYD   And your nose is pretty well hammered sideways, too . . .

CARL   It was when I was coming back from Témiscamique one time and I was crossing on the cage ferry at Deux Rivières with some horses and the Assyrian peddlar and he told me about the Devil of Chalk River — and he got it straight from the Indians.

LLOYD   When you think of it, a whole lot of this Valley is full of haunts — all around MacNabb country, White Lake, Waba, I've been there — br-r-r — that's rough — spookey feeling country . . .

CARL   And I've heard of the Witch of Plum Hollow — that Witch's house is still there — the one old Sir John A used to go to see to find out if he would win the next election.

LLOYD   The day we elect a Conservative here I'll eat your Saturday socks.

CARL   I don't believe any of that nonsense at all — we left it all behind in Ireland.

LLOYD   I've never met a man who's been to the bush and not heard the loup-garou.

CARL   Sure, I've heard the wolves howl. You can still hear them howling at the moon here — they howled and howled all night long all of them when the Petawawa paratroopers got drowned in the Ottawa.

LLOYD   They say along the river you can still hear them crying for help.

CARL   They say along the river you can still hear the drowning river-drivers crying for help — especially at Deep River there where there's no bottom to the river — and at the Swisha they swear they can still hear Danny Colton going round and round in the whirlpool there calling for help — eighteen times he went round before he went under.

LLOYD   When I was a boy I used to play in a haunted house —

CARL   Come on, you old goat! I told you I don't believe any of that stuff.

LLOYD   It was the old Shannon castle in Pembroke deserted for years and I used to visit my cousins there. Some of the Shannon tribe and old Mrs. Cassie Delahaye — she'd been a Shannon — she lived next door and she used to give us the key on Saturdays so we could play there; and oh god! It was spooky! Her husband had been killed in the First World War and she hadn't touched a thing since then — just like that mausoleum — everything exactly the way it was before he died. It was fully furnished and all the blinds were pulled — so it was always dark as a tomb — and spooky — and it was all there. All the old newspapers from World War I — and World War I pith helmets and uniforms and swords, and huge pictures of dead men and women looking down at your from the walls, and bread knives still in the drawers and bread containers so big we could climb into them and lock each other inside — and upstairs — the bed sheets were still on the beds.

CARL   People have to be crazy to keep a place like that.

LLOYD   We never got to the third floor — even on the second floor — away from the door — we'd stop talking and start tiptoeing — and listening — and hearing squeaks — and then somebody would yell, "What's that!" and we'd and we'd all turn and start running and nearly kill each other on the way out the door until the next Saturday when Mrs. Delahaye would give us the key.

CARL   You sound like them damn fool Frenchmen talking in the lumber camp about the Chaise-Galerie.

LLOYD   I was back in the bush for McCool on the old Black River when the witch-canoe came in to take all the Frenchmen home for New Year's Eve —

CARL   Lordy Blue Jesus! Why didn't you go with them!

LLOYD   Because the witch-canoe only takes Frenchmen . . .

CARL   Do you remember the banshee that came to the window before Long Jim Shea died?

LLOYD   For two weeks before he died the banshee came and looked in the window.

CARL   Oh, Lord, how Long Jim Shea could sing!

LLOYD   I've seen Telesphore Toussant, the Ghost of the Jocko River.

CARL   Tell it, you damn fool. You will anyway.

LLOYD   It was when I was up for McCool I saw his ghost — Telesphore Toussant was on old shantyman who worked for Gillies in a lumbercamp on the Jocko River. He was a terrible blasphemer and the shantymen who worked with him did not like his blasphemies at all. It was against their religion — and they used to say to him "The Lord will strike you down Telesphore, if you don't stop that blaspheming. And the one day the Lord did strike

him down and Telesphore drowned in the Jocko.
Of course, he went straight to the Devil and the
Devil told him his punishment. "You will haunt
the Jocko River for the rest of time," the Devil told
old Telesphore. And for sometime after that the
ghost of Telesphore haunted the Gillies
lumbercamp. The shantymen said that at night he
often came into the sleep camp through the roof.
But after that the lumbercamp all fell into ruins
and Toussant had nowhere to go but to the shores
of the Jocko River — and that's where he wanders
yet — and that's where I saw his ghost. I was with
Norman Sheehand. He can tell you . . .

POET   All around Arnprior
and Flat Rapids
the old lads
still say Allan Dhu
killed Indian girls

the Last Laird MacNab's
illegitimate son
by Catherine "Granny" Fisher,
they still say Allan Dhu
killed Indian girls

"he lay in wait
in the roadside ditches
and along the shore
of the River"

the old lads at White Lake,
Lochwinnoch, Waba,
they still say Allan Dhu
killed Indian girls

ask them how,
none will answer

ask them how many,
nobody knows

ask them how he died
nobody tells.

CARL   They're playing games at Petawawa today — the boys have brought up the big cannons — all the windows have been shaking all morning.

LLOYD   Tommy Barnett died the other day in Renfrew — the last of the timber baron's sons.

CARL   The kitchen is emptying out — emptying out.

LLOYD   I mean to be a long time here yet.

CARL   I've had a good long life —

LLOYD   And made a lot of women happy.

CARL   Yes, as Tessie the Trapper used to say, "Thank God for your cock! Thank God for your cock!"

LLOYD   If you were that good, you would have been dead long ago.

CARL   Yes, a long good life — but I might have one regret.

LLOYD   What might that be?

CARL   I wish I'd joined up.

LLOYD And if you had you might have been playing the dead part of your life a long time now.

CARL The closest I ever come to seeing what war can do was when Dan Culhane was blown up in the Sudbury mine. Put his drill in a hole with a piece of live dynamite. And they took him home in a matchbox to bury him in Calabogie.

LLOYD Well, after the next one there'll be nobody left around to put any of us in matchboxes.

CARL I was too young to join in the First World War —

LLOYD I couldn't leave me poor mother alone on the farm —

CARL God! Remember when the bush here used to be full of them hiding out — all the Frenchmen — and all the Irishmen — who wouldn't fight the "English" wars. All the lads from Mount St. Patrick and Pakenham, the Burnt Lands of Huntley, Sheenboro —

LLOYD Oh, yes, it was too young — too colour blind — we all were.

CARL Father Hunt — old Tom Hunt used to always tell that story about Mrs. Mulligan meeting Mrs. Corrigan on the street in Eganville and Mrs. Mulligan says, "Oh, Mrs. Corrigan, I just got a fine letter from my son in London. He has got himself a great job entirely."
 "And what might that be?" Mrs Corrigan asks.
 "Sure, he's working in a crematorium," says Mrs. Mulligan.

"And what's so wonderful about that?" says Mr. Corrigan.

"Sure he'd burning up Englishmen and getting paid for it!" says Mrs. Mulligan.

LLOYD   Well, I've often heard Father Harrington tell about the time he got that phone call from Ottawa, from some English captain there, a damn recruiting officer and he says to Father Harrington, "Father, I'm coming up the line tomorrow to investigate — the Chapeau boys don't seem to be joining up in any great numbers at all." And Father Harrington roars into the phone, "Well, come ahead. Come ahead." And the Blightie says, "My goodness, father! I didn't expect you to roar such a welcome for me!" And Father Harrington says, "Come ahead, come ahead. But you'd better bring a pine box with you." And the English Officer says, "And for what exactly would I be needing a pine box?" "Well," roars Father Harrington into the phone, "you won't be needing it on the way up here but you'll damn well be needing it on the way back . . . "

CARL   Father Regan down there at Fort Colonge — he went even further — he used to ring the church bells — four shorts — every time the recruiting officer was coming up the line.

LLOYD   That's right, I'd almost forgotten about that.

CARL   Well, one time this young Army Officer — I think it was a Gervais — came home to Fort Coulonge on leave — and he only had a couple of days and he wanted his son baptized while he was home and Father Regan agreed to do it in a hurry and the young officer was so pleased to get it all done so

quickly he gave the Holy Father a fifty dollar bill
— and Father Regan was so excited he went out to
ring the church bell — he rang the wrong ones —
four shorts — and all the draft dodgers — my god
they all leaped from their beds and out through
windows and down the streets, some of them half-
dressed and took to the woods for another spell of
time. Yes — and think of all the Chapeau boys that
did join up.

LLOYD   And never came back —

CARL   Well, they say nobody will come back from the
next one.

LLOYD   Nobody. We're sitting at the end of the last of the
good times.

CARL   Yup — nice big kitchen — sitting here between
the Boys Playing Games at Petawawa and the Boys
Playing Games at Chalk River.

LLOYD   I was up river the other day with Tex Naves to the
Swisha and you know when you get to Chalk River
you can see all that heavy water coming into the
Ottawa — black and fat and bloated.

CARL   Well, you know why they picked Chalk River?

LLOYD   No, why?

CARL   Well, I learned this from the Indians — you know I
lived with the Indians? Well, I lived with the
Indians and this goes back to way before Columbus
sailed the ocean blue.

LLOYD In 1642!

CARL But back since before the beginning of whatever the hell it is we have here — the Indians of Chalk River would never hunt around Chalk River. They wouldn't even paddle on the river. They wouldn't go anywhere near it. And do you know why?

LLOYD Why?

CARL Because they said it was haunted. Yes, haunted by a Devil in a flaming ball of fire — with an open hand in the middle of it.

LLOYD An open hand in the middle of it — well, you know I only went as far as the blackboard in school.

CARL And I only went three rainy days.

LLOYD But I've always wondered why they go to university for degrees — and then cook up something as stupid as an atomic bomb.

CARL Nothing better to do, I guess. It's like some of them Department of Forestry men who come up here to give us advice on my timber — five degrees in trees and they don't know a white pine from a turkey in heat.

LLOYD Oh, god I heard a great one the other day! Toddy Murphy back there in the Nickabeau on that old homestead of theirs back in the bush sold a bunch of log buildings — square timber — to some bigwig — some professor from Ottawa U — and he sent

up the log experts and he told them to take them
apart and he told them to be sure to number the
logs — and by the holy fathers of Mount St.
Patrick, do you know what they did?

CARL   What?

LLOYD   They took all the buildings apart — and then they
numbered the logs !
(They roll on the ground laughing)

CARL   We'll have to have another beer on that one.

LLOYD   Well, nobody will come back from the next one.

CARL   I've had a good long life — doesn't matter to me —
if they blow everything up — no kids — no wife —

LLOYD   That may have been our big mistake.

CARL   "Never tie a knot with your tongue . . ."

LLOYD   When that plane went down with Kathleen at the
Pembroke Fair — I stopped singing for a year —

CARL   Only one woman I ever loved — Chantal Tessier
— when I was working at Paugeen Falls in the
Gatineau she was a teacher there — I met her at
church in Ste. Cécile de Masham — then I went
off to diamond-drill near Sudbury and she was
waiting for me — and I came back with all the
money saved to get married — and she was dead —
died of appendicitis — I lay on her grave for two
days and then I got up — I haven't given a good
goddamn for anything since —

Music   "I'll take you home again Kathleen . . . "

POET   When I first heard the strange bawling in the far fields
of his cousin's farms I thought of a cow going down
in quick-sand, or hoisted on thorns, and I was all ready
to ride to the rescue of a dumb animal. But Carl laughed.
"I've heard them go on like that for two or three days
after the calves are taken to market." And this morning,
horses knee-deep and crushing the wild strawberries underfoot,
the barn swallows, climbing frenzy, are weaving in and out
of the woodshed where the nest was knocked down
and the eggs smashed on the pine boards of the old floor.

Watching them I think of the Death Notice in the Globe
and Mail yesterday, a young man, nineteen, killed in the Rockies
(trying to fly without wings, no doubt) and his parents
quoting Isaiah — "Lo, I have carved thee on the palms
of my hands." Meanwhile, *these* grieving mates, the swallows
continue to do unswallow-like things; they squawk
like crows, chirp like sparrows, fly stumblingly
through the trees at the woodshed door as though grief,
grooven deep enough, will black out instinct and direction.

Now and again, as the perfect June day fan-fans out,
the swallows in disbelief swoop back into the woodshed
to the high beam (Oh, not high enough!) they chose together
so carefully upon their returning last April to a country
somewhat north of Capistrano and there, miscalculating
their enemy and the mask upon his heart, they sang,
made love, built and, in a mite moment of joy,
without language or hands, gave life to life.

But it is true. The broken nest, the white, the yolks
of eggs, all is lying on the pine boards of the old woodshed.

Verily, a miracle of resurrection would be more easily grasped
than this fact of destruction! Then in and out, back and forth
iridescence fading in the sunlight, their sharp eyes graying
towards noon, they continue pacing the sky, round and round,
calling out to one another faintly as mice midair
but unable to share this burden not in the Books of their Bible
larger than their tiny bodies, heavier than family.

They are lost. What is the reason now left for flying?
How shall the barns have swallows next year, and next,
to keep them safe from infestations and emptiness?
Where shall the summer sky on the bona fide farm
wear that wringing wreath of bright reassuring continuity?
Was not this nest an anchor holding the world together?

All day June the swallows mourn for their dead unborn
and guard the demeaned dwelling-place of love.
By eventide when the hungry Red-Tail comes low and punctual
out of the pine forest to hunt in the fields, they are gone,
gone to wherever it is that birds go to die of grief,
gone to wherever it is that birds go to begin again.
The woodshed returns to wood.

Cavan, pragmatic unmated, imperviously childless,
does not understand why he struck out this way,
yea, no more than we understand the soul of a cow,
the grief of barn swallow, or the reasons why we,
Isaiah's misbegotten, continue making missiles.

SECTION 6 *Endings*

WOMAN I Stand at the ruins
of any great timber-slide
along the River
you'll see their bravado
ghost go by.

Chain-lightning Stewart,
Cock-eye George McNee,
Gentleman Paddy Dillon,
King of the Madawaska

search in the undergrowth
of any of the rapids
along the River
you'll find the rough-hewn crosses
of the river-drivers' graves

(Gerry Garneau from the Gaspé
was caught in a centre-jam,
and a two-ton stick took out
the Tessier lad
from St. Cécile de Masham)

TOM MURRAY I knew back in 1890 when I was digging potatoes
for my father on the Opeongo Line at home there
that I would never be a farmer. I said to myself,
"Tom Murray, you'll never be a farmer" And I went
into lumber with the first dollar I saved. It's a
strange thing you know, the Murray brothers
lumbering was a minor operation. But we're the
only ones in the whole Ottawa Valley that lasted
and lasted. Where, oh where, are the sons of the

Big lumbermen of yesteryear. The Barnetts, the
Hales, the Booths, the Dunlops, the McLachlins!
Oh God! The sons of the lumbermen! There's not
even one of them left! Pembroke had about six big
lumber companies and there's none left. I used to
go down to Pembroke sixty-five years ago and go
into the hotels there. Full of lumbermen and sons
of lumbermen. The Mackies were big then. And
they were great big men, too. Tom Mackie was six
foot six. And look at J.R. Booth; he had nobody to
carry on his business. And when Second Day
McLachlin died, there weren't any young
McLachlins that were able to handle that business
— and the Barnetts just faded out — yessir there
are two most unfortunate things that can happen
in life; it is most unfortunate for a young woman to
be born too good-looking and it is most
unfortunate for a young man to be born too rich.

WOMAN 1   And Old Tom Murray
was never in a hurry
to die at Barry's Bay

MAN 2   At one hundred and one
he said to his second son,
"As true as I'm sitting here today
my mother was the smartest woman
that ever peeled
a twelve-quart pail
of old potatoes
with just her thumb-nail,

"And I'll be pleased to tell you right off
the only reason I am living so long
is, yes, I was born in the bush
in a cedar sap-trough,

"And the second reason,
come to think of it,
is one that you've heard
many times before —
in all my live-long life
I've never lifted the latch
on a Protestant church door."

WOMAN I   Old Tom Murray
was never in a hurry
to die at Barry's Bay

and for all the right reasons
he's living there today.

POET   this a picture of my grandfather Hodgins
himself   he was a very important person
he made this country   how he sat on his stoop
in the evening and looked over his fattening fields
harmonized with the hills and the emerging
night-hawks   in his time   which was very early
he fenced seven hundred acres   to some of his six sons
coming of age in Pontiac County he gave farms nearby
I learned the love of the land from him at the farm
he never spoke it aloud once but it was his eyes
travelling over the timothy and oats that taught me
pride   his praise was silent and something
to be reckoned with as was his given word
all church sermons suffered from the eloquence
in the pit of his eyes   in his eighties I sat
at his feet and read to him and when he took up
his cane I knew we would go together to the barns
what unfolded in me was that we have nothing
to fear from belonging to the universe
and that there is nothing so gentle as strength

I was not the only one who loved him you know
when he died in the late thirties I stood
at the kitchen window knowing that even
the wind on the farm would never be the same again
and counted eighty-five cars following
his coffin to the little graveyard at Radford

his prized stallion, Dark Thunder, dropped dead
in his stall the very next day   the windmill quit
and Sounder crawled in under the carriage shed
and stayed there   as quickly as they could
his lane of maples died of nothing to live for

like a stunned animal my grandmother reeled
through the remainder of her days   her chest
became hollow   her silk hair turned to straw
she became a whisper in the rooms   in November
she got all his clothes ready for his annual trip
to the Winter Fair   laid out on the bed
his worsted suit, good tie, starched white shirt
giant beaver hat and coat   smiled a little daft
and elfin smile when they reminded her of where
he was   it is far too late for me to learn
to live without him   she said   and put her head
down on the kitchen table for a cat-nap   the way
she used to do when there were fifteen hired men
coming in for dinner along with her family of ten

there are no photographs of my grandmother Hodgins
extant   they say happy women have no history.

MAN I   All the sons of the Valley
        of the Twenty-Six Rivers
        cross over, cross over
        cross over the Chapeau Bridge

gone to southern cities
in search of pensions
and appliances
and a "nice safe cage"

they have left behind them
a relayered Wilderness.

MAN I   Our Valley forefathers
they sleep now on quiet hills
who carried wheat on their backs
to be ground
at far away mills

this land was their land
by right of guts and sweat
and this the softened sons
of sons forget.

POET   As I have never
come from the fields
without flowers

So I have never
come from your presence
without the understanding
of love

and there is no poem
to be written
after this
one.

Songs from Both Sides of the River *was commissioned by the National Arts Centre in Ottawa. In 1986 dramaturge Maureen Labonté read some of my recent love poetry and arranged for a workshop reading in the Great Canadian Theatre. Gil Osborne, then working as a producer at the Arts Centre, heard the workshop reading and offered me a contract to write a play set in the Ottawa Valley, "a kind of Under Milkwood," she said. The play ran for two weeks in the fall of 1987 to sold-out houses, with a cast of actors including Rebecca Campbell, Windi Dawson, Heather Esdon, Gerald Lunz, and Robert Welch. Gil Osborne directed the play, with set design by Don Finlayson and musical soundscape by James Stephens. James Stephens and Randy Hughson performed the music, with songs written by Paul Bontineau, Nathan Curry, Reg Hill, and Jean Carignan, and researched by Nathan Curry. The stage manager was Laura Kennedy. Maureen Labonté was the dramaturge. Plans to tour the play throughout the Valley were never fulfilled.*

Part Four

The Breakwater and the Web

The Breakwater and the Web

The returning. The returning when the need
for the Valley rises in you like desire
for a man who has cherished you;
The returning to find so many more
have gone underground, but the few remaining
still sharing the same unspoken passion
for the landscape as breakwater, as anodyne,
as Sunday sermon, as restoration, as a soul-song
we all retain in the same "hearing ear."

Weddings, births, illnesses, funerals
all excuses for returning to restore my being
with belonging in the web; to hear
some ancient uncle recite the genealogy
as historians The Kings;
it gives you power to know that Alfie Harper
married Bertha, the third McAdam sister
from below Quyon — hear how he says it? —
and Averina Smart married first a Hodgins
from out back, a second cousin to be exact,
and, when he died, an Armstrong from The Front,
both gimpy-legged men but strong in the arms.

My great-great-great grandparents here
in Pontiac County, in Quebec, in Canada,
not exiles but immigrants, not forced
by starvation out of an emerald county
despoiled by black potatoes, not shipped
by absentee landlords to the stony shores
of their native land and ordered
to leave — or die.

No. Choosers. The reins of their lives
in their hands. And I carry their decision
in my genes as surely as the moments
of conception; they were benevolent royalty;
they held sway by sweat; they walked as Lords
of the Land, sometimes shaking their heads
in disbelief at the reign of their good fortunes,
sometimes living to see stricken offspring
betray their newfound kingdom
of hope and glory.

The early network of Valley clans held me,
rocked me in a hammock, every web of the rope
protecting my flesh, every interstice my spirit.
"Lo! I am with you always" scripted in gold lettering
on the cream walls of Boyneville United Church
had for me, forced prisoner fidgeting
in the Elliot pew, nothing to do with a God
but only with all people who loved me
and whom, at my mother's knee, I remembered
in my childhood prayers as I laid me down to sleep.

Later, it only had to do with all the people
I loved who betrayed and abandoned me,
and I no longer believed in prayers;
in this way, I was always less than my mother
who, no matter how often tragedy bowed
her brave head, continued praying
(and cursing) to the end.

The hired men on my grandfather's Valley farm,
Pontiac County, Province of Quebec, Country of Canada,
came from nowhere and went to nowhere and when
we were sent to get the mail, got no mail;
and I couldn't believe they could do
such a long hard hot day's work in the midst
of all that belonging to nowhere, and to nobody.

Nobody to care enough to tell you time for bed,
nobody to hear your voice and what you were really saying,
nobody to tell you to put on your Sunday clothes,
get your hair shingled, nobody to pry open your mouth,
order you to say "ah," and then paint your tonsils
with turpentine.

But there was one hired man we called Uncle Joe;
he used to sit on the kitchen stoop steps
and sing songs from his country he said
was far far away across the Atlantic Ocean;
he was a Barnardo Boy, and he never left the farm
to go to nowhere like the other hired men.
He stayed. And lived in the attic all his life
while across the Atlantic Ocean his network
of clans was dying off without him
ever getting word. No. Nobody ever said
of Uncle Joe as they did of all the neighbours
and relatives, "He got word yesterday in the mail.
or, "There was a telegram. His brother
passed away in Ballysadare."

And you, in your wisdom,
whom do you want to be present
at your death?

And who, in their wisdom,
will be there?

In childhood everywhere we went in the Valley
the arms held us, and wise men patted us on the head,
knowing what we would become by the shape of our eyes;
old wise women knew from watching for so long
what was in our genes — "a Harper temper,"
"a cowlick from the Cuthbertsons," "pray God
the drink doesn't come down from the Finnigans,"
"that one's all Caldwell," "the ears are pure Murray."

And we stood still, like cattle being judged
at the Boyneville Fair, feeling uncomfortable
because we sensed the judges knew our destiny —
some for work, and some for war, some for racing,
some for breeding, some marked for a return
to the wilds or an early death, some to wander
forever between two worlds, and only a few
for true love.

Oh, I'd read all about the begats in the Bible —
Genesis, Exodus, Leviticus, Numbers, Deuteronomy;
True, they were Jewish begats — I knew that —
but it was the Valley begats that bound me
into the tribe, that established a network
that was to cover the country, up and down
both sides of the Ottawa River, Ontario and Quebec,
and over all the mountains, Gatineau, Opeongo.

My wizened hard-done-by great-grandmother Murray —
"Old Dick drank everything away, you know" —
spoke French in her house on Booth Street in Ottawa,
and my Algonquin Indian ancestor on Calumet Island
was successfully hidden under the tribal rug
for years until some people began to think
perhaps it was the White Man who was "Le Sauvage."

So, although I was always on the outside,
I was never alone; there was a Hodgins relation
lurking everywhere, filling up the Valley
since that very first day when "Daddy Tom"
in with the survey crew from Quebec City,
sighted "The Springs" at Boyneville and remembered
the country he had left behind him,
a vision of Galway from the Sky Road
stuck in his throat.

The Harpers and the Caldwells, on the other hand,
did not have the Hodgins prolificity in their loins;
they were simply big men, used to hoisting
hay-ricks, enemies and horses; and two Harper lads
married two Caldwell sisters, creating —
it was always said — the branch known
to this very day as the "Hanging Harpers."

Yes, in the Valley, if you fell in love again,
almost always it was into the honey-pot of incest;
you sometimes had to leave the Valley, go west
to clear the strain or, if you couldn't leave,
then declare there was "no one good enough
to marry"; that's why the Valley eventually
was full of old Irish bachelors and spinsters
snarling at one another, and dying without wills.

On the Quebec side, back in the Nickabeau,
a tribe evolved with fish-scales on their hands.

On my Radford grandfather's farm
summer thunderstorms allowed no one to sleep,
not my night-prowling young uncles,
not the hired men,
not me.

Summer storms, it was always said, were sent
from the mountains on the Ontario side of the River
into the pure Irish bailiwicks of Western Quebec,
lambasting, psychopathic annihilating
Canadian rains, spiked with thunder
and lightening, flattening the good grain,
setting the hay barns on fire,
striking dead the hired men
sheltering under the elm trees
in the arm fields
taking down windmills,
snapping off lightning rods,
sending the women into fiddlings
of fear and recitations of all the deaths
by lightning occurring in the Valley
for the last hundred years
on both sides of the River.

Valley rain was not the soft civilized rain
of Ireland, fairy-footed, caressing
forty shades of green, tapping
at Queen Maeve's tomb
on top of Knocknarea.

Valley rain was not an Irish rain
gently falling through court tombs,
ruined castles and monasteries,
gently pelting O'Rourke's Table
and the lovers last picnic there
before Diarmid MacMurrough came
to carry off Dervorgilla.

No, it was the savage rain
of a big adolescent half-grown country
and in my Valley clan the women went haywire,
especially if the storm came at night;
I had one evangelical aunt who used
to rouse everyone in the house,
seat them at the kitchen table
and lead them in prayer
for the duration of the storm,
raising her arms heavenwards
chorusing "Hallelujah!"
at every clap of thunder,
every bolt of lightning.

On the Radford farm it wasn't the thunderstorm,
it was my grandmother who terrified me;
She lit the lamps, wakened everyone
and started moving the bedroom furniture
all around the room,
away from the big bay window,
trying to outrun the lightning.

I can see her yet, her long braid flying,
pushing the marital bed on its casters
from wall to wall, massive decorated
iron and brass, into the corner,
away from the window, back to the wall,
wheel around again, now back and forth
in a whimpering frenzy,
until finally she set me off
and I joined in her hysteria,
I who, in the city in my father's house,
was a rain-worshipper,
I who knew the parameters
of my drought.

My grandfather would follow his wife
around the bedroom, trying to pacify her
as he would a frightened horse
on the road or in the barn,
and finally one time,
fed up, to calm my fears
took me into bed with him.

And after that when I visited
the Radford farm,
I slept with my grandfather.

We walked to the Auditorium on Argyle Street
to watch our father play, untrippable right wing,
star for the Ottawa Senators, top scorer,
captain of the team, idol of the Twenties;
and we all carried home to the house on McLeod Street,
and further into our dreams and our roaring out,
chorus and command, "We want Finnigan!"
"We want Finnigan!"

We skated every day, every night, all weekend
on a dozen outdoor neighbourhood rinks,
and built ice igloos in the backyard
so big my mother used to be afraid
we would get lost in them, or have to be rescued
from cave-ins. Revelling in winter, we were
to be fastened to the rhythms of ice forming
and snow falling forever.

Before school began in the fall, we had
wild cucumber fights up and down the spooky lanes
between the houses on our street, over the fences,
through the neighbours' backyards, down the alleys,
armed with the oozy prickly green fruit of the vine,
squealing with delight and satisfaction
when a direct aim splattered or pin-cushioned
someone on the enemy side.

And all the backyards in Centretown
(even the rich Armstong's next door to us),
having been household garbage dumps for years,
yielded up to little skipping girls
treasures of broken glass, green, purple,
blue, orange, for the hours of hopscotching
unmolested on the sidewalks of our city,
when only the Lindberg child
was ever kidnapped.

And my father, after he had sung "We are poor little lambs"
in teary drunkenness at the kitchen table,
would sound out over Centretown
into the listening midnight,
"Alcohol is a pain-killer used by people
who don't know where their pain is."
And I lay upstairs with my head under my pillow,
and wished to God someone would put him out of his pain,
and knew he needed help with his pain.

The next morning, his head hanging,
contrite, begging for another chance,
he would be faced with my mother,
her mouth set in evangelical moral judgment,
nagging at him, preaching at him,
"Parents who are still children
cannot raise children."

It took me years and years to figure out
why she chose him; and why she stayed.

My Aunt Bessie always used to say,
"The worst kind of lies
are not mouthed, but lived."
After she died, and they found
the love letters, we knew
she was talking about herself.

"Over-watered grain
is just as damaged as drought-grain."
That was a favourite of my Uncle Archie's
who owned a farm three down the Back Road
from my Radford grandfather. I pondered
that one for years but fortunately
had it figured out before
I had my own children.

When I was sixteen, Amy Lowell,
the New England poet,
yelled out at me,
"Christ! What are patterns for?"
But I already knew that good patterns
are for using again,
and sick patterns for breaking.

Joan Finnigan

In the web of my Valley clans
there are many drought-children,
those who had enough sustenance
to survive physically but never enough
to mature emotionally.

For the outsider, the drought-children
are difficult to identify (and therefore avoid)
because they come in so many disguises —
the narcissistic beauty, the eternal stage-player,
the neurotic creator, the charming prover,
the frigid intellectual, the superman,
the unmateable woman, the driven power-seeker,
the secret perfectionist, the masked fanatic,
the punitive parent —

Only those very close to me knew my disguises
and, very young, sensing my deficiencies,
I became a rain-worshipper;
when the city was lambasted
with a savage summer deluge,
sometimes bombarding hailstones,
I used to sit out, alone,
on the upstairs verandah
and drink it in.
There was never enough Valley rain
to end my drought.

We were always learning about dying
and how we should go about it;
slowly with curses and passion,
taking the time to relent and forgive,
like saintly Aunt Jessica
who had so little to forgive;
or instantly, as cousin Silas,
like a military jet tearing
the summer skies apart,
without time to look back,
or into the eyes of a loved one,
without time to ask
that anything be forgiven.

Even when I was young
I always said that I would return to the Valley
when I was old, go down to the River
for my death; and I am doing that,
just that, circling, circling like the hawk
over the meadow, like the osprey over the lake,
taking my time in my two worlds,
coming in for a landing.

Joan Finnigan

He dies easy who, in his life,
loved something, some place
someone more than life;
in this way he understands
that death is simply
part of life,
as love is the breakwater
of the universe
and the web.

Printed in Canada